Pause.
Breathe.
Flourish.

Living Your Best Life
as an Educator

William D. Parker

ConnectEDD Publishing
Chicago, Illinois

This publication is available at discount pricing when purchased in quantity for educational purposes, promotions, or fundraisers. For inquiries and details, contact the publisher at:
info@connecteddpublishing.com

Published by ConnectEDD Publishing LLC
Chicago, IL
www.connecteddpublishing.com

Cover Design: Kheila Dunkerly

Pause. Breathe. Flourish: Living Your Best Life as an Educator/ William D. Parker. —1st ed.
Paperback ISBN: 978-1-7348908-4-6
Ebook ISBN: 978-1-7348908-5-3

Praise for *Pause. Breathe. Flourish.*

When I first met Will Parker at an education conference, I was struck immediately by his open, compassionate, honest approach to everything from raising children to mentoring educators. That same genuineness infuses every page of *Pause. Breathe. Flourish.*, a practical, inspiring guide to education leadership—and to living a good, meaningful life. Readers will appreciate Parker's willingness to share times when he stumbled, along with lessons he learned. He recognizes the unique challenges that educators face, from navigating loneliness, to making tough decisions, to asking for help, to carving out time for faith, friendship, and family. He provides specific tips to help educators manage time effectively, share knowledge with others, stay fresh intellectually, bolster mental strength and maintain perspective, prioritize relationships and physical health, and leave a strong legacy. If that sounds like a tall order, it is, but Parker pulls it off as only he can—with grace and humility. Every educator should read *Pause. Breathe. Flourish.*

—**Phyllis L. Fagell**, LCPC, School Counselor, Author of *Middle School Matters*, and Washington Post journalist

In his book *Pause. Breathe. Flourish.*, Will Parker reflects on his life and experiences as he creatively encourages us to reflect on our own education leadership practices. He provides educators with a personal look at leadership supported by research and sound practices that creates a balance for leading and living. A must read for early career and veteran educators who will find support and encouragement on their journey.

—**Jayne Ellspermann,** School Leadership Development Consultant, 2015 NASSP National Principal of the Year

In *Pause. Breathe. Flourish.*, William D. Parker helps us lift our eyes from the everyday challenges of education, and develop a long-term vision for our well-being and impact. In a world where educators are often called upon to sacrifice their personal health, time, and relationships for the sake of school needs, Parker's book is a wake-up call that our greatest impact comes *as a result of*—not in spite of—our investment in ourselves. Highly recommended for teachers, school leaders, principal preparation faculty, aspiring leaders, and senior leaders who supervise educators.

> —**Justin Baeder, PhD**, Director of The Principal Center & author of *Now We're Talking! 21 Days to High-Performance Instructional Leadership*

There are few voices I listen to in education, but one that I find consistently genuine and inspiring is the voice of Will Parker. In *Pause. Breathe. Flourish.*, Will shares a generous book, weaving together personal anecdotes with practical advice and next steps for educators. I often tell others, 'You can't pour from an empty cup.' This book will fill you up so that you are able to be the servant leader you were born to be.

> —**Daniel Bauer**, Chief Ruckus Maker at Better Leaders Better Schools

Will Parker has done it again. In a personal fashion, he's laid out a plan for self-care. His words are relevant, down to earth, and practical. His tips are doable for any educator. If you're in need of feeding yourself before you feed anyone else, this book is for you. Especially, in the midst of this crazy year, *Pause. Breathe. Flourish.* will provide you the fundamentals you need to live well and lead well.

> —**Dr. Tim Elmore**, Founder, CEO of GrowingLeaders.com

Will Parker was my principal in high school. It was there that I learned his passion and dedication to education that shines through in *Pause. Breathe. Reflect.* As an educator, he encouraged and supported me. Now, as a young professional reading his latest book, I appreciate his honest advice about sacrifice and finding joy in the crazy balance we call life. I believe Parker's words are applicable to every professional, regardless of the field, and will provide inspiration to educators young and old.

—**Lily Cummings**, Reporter, Multimedia Journalist, Tulsa, Oklahoma

In Will Parker's book, *Pause. Breathe. Flourish. Living Your Best Life as An Educator*, I found myself reconnecting to the power of self-reflection and most importantly how it can effectively influence my perspective in school leadership. Whether you are a new or experienced educator, you will find connections in leadership experiences through his career and personal narratives in the guiding steps and questions found in the book's 'Now It's Your Turn' feature.

—**Sonia Lopez-Morales**, San Antonio ISD - Graebner Elementary

Pause. Breathe. Flourish. is a step-by-step guide on self-care for educators. It is a must read for any school administrator opening a school during this global pandemic and racial awakening. Will Parker reminds us that as school leaders we have the responsibility to take care of ourselves first. If we don't make self-care a priority in our lives, we will then have nothing left for the important work of supporting our staff."

—**Brighid M. Gates**, Principal, B.M. Williams Primary School, Chesapeake, VA

Will Parker's book *Pause. Breathe. Flourish.* comes at a perfect time. It's often a challenge for educators to balance work responsibilities while making time to take care for themselves and their loved ones. During this time when educators are being asked to create safe schools in the midst of a pandemic, we are facing new challenges daily and often feeling overwhelmed. Parker's guide to a balanced approach to work and life offers practical strategies and asks important questions educators can reflect on to identify how to eliminate unnecessary stress during these challenging times.

—**LaDonna Chancellor**, Principal, Bartlesville High School, Bartlesville, Oklahoma

As an educator, colleague, and friend, I have the opportunity to work with Will Parker on a daily basis. Will lives what he writes. His reflections on his life experiences are organized in a thoughtful compilation of guided questions that touch all aspects of our lives with action steps and challenges to help us be our best selves. Like Will, this book is genuine in its goal to help others. We can see ourselves as educators through his eyes and his experiences. I highly recommend this book and the advice he offers: pause and breathe so that you can flourish in your personal and professional life.

—**Dr. Pam Deering**, Executive Director, Cooperative Council for Oklahoma School Administration, Oklahoma Association of School Administrators

In *Pause. Breathe. Flourish.*, Will Parker shares the difficulties educators have tending to their own physical, mental, and spiritual health, but why it is so important to prioritize these. There is a quote that says, "Good people are like candles; they burn themselves up to give others light." This is true, but Will provides practical strategies and expert insight on how educators can give light to others without burning themselves up, by intentionally refueling their passions. This book is a must read for any educator who needs to find balance and tip the scales of health, wealth and prosperity in their favor.

—**Dr. Don Parker**, principal, speaker, author of *Building Bridges: Engaging Students At-Risk Through the Power of Relationships*

Dedication

This book is dedicated to my parents, Jesse Darden Parker, Sr., and Polly Kathryn Carter Parker. From my earliest memories, they have encouraged me to use my gifts, to chase my dreams, and to trust in God above all else. Their words, actions, and wisdom have helped me to appreciate the small beauties in life and discover the joy of contentment—whether during life's storms or blessings.

Foreword

I had no idea that this book would be published during one of the most pivotal moments in the history of modern education. 2020 has brought us a global pandemic, worldwide marches with calls to eradicate racism, and surreal political debates. This year has been fraught with challenges and opportunities larger than what many educators have ever faced. Each moment has been accompanied by images we will never forget: Educators wearing masks and gloves to protect students from air-borne viruses. People of every age and background marching in the streets with cries of "I can't breathe," to memorialize the tragic death of George Floyd and to call for social justice. Politicians and government officials agonizing over the balance between public health and re-opening schools and businesses. A little-known fact: books are begun long before they ever become published works. I began this book in 2017. Like my other books, this one came as a response to questions I was receiving from other educators. As I have presented to educators across the nation on ways to achieve meaningful outcomes within school communities, I have consistently heard this question: "With so many demands as an educator, how do I take care of my own individual growth and health?"

Questions like this require honest conversation. Although *Pause. Breathe. Flourish.* was written before the seismic shifts of 2020 began, I believe it has universal application for educators. In the pages ahead, you will discover how your thoughts, relationships, commitments, values, and habits play an essential role in who you are as a person. And 'who you are' plays heavily in your ability to weather storms, maintain perspective, work with purpose and effect meaningful change in your own life and in the lives of others. I hope this book finds you in a time less stressful than the months we have all experienced during the global pandemic. But my guess is that you are already managing another time of difficulty or challenge. As you do, may you find the lessons ahead ones that can add perspective and help you flourish along the way.

Pause.
Breathe.
Flourish.

*Living Your Best Life
as an Educator*

William D. Parker

Table of Contents

Pause.
Breathe.
Flourish.

Preface

Your Self-Care: When a Crisis Hits, Who Breathes First?

The Oxygen Mask: *This is a common danger for educators. So often, as we are caring for others, we fail to care for ourselves first. In the process, we may not have the necessary strength, wisdom, or insight to help those whom we are supposed to be serving.*

I'm a frequent flyer. The more I fly, the harder I find it is to stay focused when flight attendants review the safety procedures. They could be standing right in front of me with the safety cards in hand, but I've heard the information so many times, I usually think about something else.

However, I seem to pay more attention when the attendant says, "If the cabin loses air pressure, an oxygen mask will drop from above your seat. Place the oxygen mask on yourself first before assisting your child or other passengers."

It's always at this point, that I think about a hard conversation I had with my wife the second year I was in school administration. One night after the kids were in bed, my wife, Missy, asked if we could talk. I had just opened my laptop to read some work emails, so I set it aside and said, "Sure. What's up?"

"The kids and I have decided that you are a dad and husband on the weekends only." She said this without any bitterness or resentment in her voice. Just simple resignation. Then she looked me in the eyes. "Will, I think you are a shell of the man you used to be."

It was difficult to hear because her words so accurately described my state of life. After eleven years as a classroom teacher, I had made the transition into the office as an assistant principal in a high school with 1,400 students. One of my goals was to be the kind of administrator I had admired and dreamed of having when I was a classroom teacher. I wanted to be the person whom teachers and students could look to for answers, solutions, and support.

I woke up early every morning to check emails and plan out my day—hours before school even began. I skipped lunches or ate quickly so that I could respond to emails or manage important situations. I supervised, observed, counseled, and evaluated. I attended after-school games and activities. And when I came home late each night, I'd fall asleep while trying to read bedtime stories to our four small children. When everyone was finally asleep, I'd stay up late to answer emails or plan for upcoming events or meetings.

In my new role, I had stopped exercising. I had gained too much weight. Frankly, my wife was right: I was a shell of the man I had once been. Each day, the pressure of serving students, teachers, and parents weighed so heavily on me that I didn't think I could sacrifice time on less important to-dos like eating right, exercising, or spending extra time with my family or in reflection.

My Letter of Resignation

When my wife went to bed the night of our important talk, I opened my laptop. Instead of working on emails, I made a decision. I wrote a letter of resignation. I explained all the reasons I would need to leave my position—how my priorities were no longer correct and how I had neglected my family and personal health. I printed the letter, put it in a file folder, and took it to my office the next morning.

When I sat down at my desk, I placed the folder on the desk's corner where I could see it at all times. And I made a commitment: I was either going to find a better way to serve my school while also caring for myself and my family, or I was resigning and changing professions.

That day was a turning point for me. I didn't discover a silver bullet. My pressures didn't change either. Instead, I found some longer-lasting solutions. I began taking small steps toward making time for other areas of my life: my family, my mind, my personal budget, my spiritual growth, and my physical health.

> When you take time to invest in areas of your life outside of work, you find more creativity, inspiration, and joy in serving others.

Over the days and years ahead, I made commitments to leave school earlier so I could be home for dinner. I started running again and working on my fitness. I started eating lunch with colleagues and laughing more. And as a result, I discovered something: When you take time to invest in areas of your life outside of work, you find more creativity, inspiration, and joy in serving others. In fact, I found my ability to connect with others, find solutions, and reach goals increased as I took the time to take care of myself first.

Self-Reflection for Educators

If you are leading a classroom, school, team, or organization, let me ask you an important question. When is the last time you reflected on the foundational values, beliefs, and motivations for why you are serving others? Just like those airline attendants tell us when we fly, you can't help others if you're not first taking care of yourself.

One of the best ways to practice putting on your own oxygen mask is by giving yourself permission for self-reflection. Self-reflection allows you to focus on ideas and thoughts that you can turn into powerful actions, which later become productive habits. And one powerful way to do that is by using images as a launching point—just like thinking about an oxygen mask may help you to think about your need for self-care.

It may come as no surprise that most educators feel overwhelmed, overworked, and overcommitted. An educator's job often involves putting out situational fires, responding to urgent needs, or satisfying the requests of a multitude of stakeholders. It's no wonder that educators, in particular, must battle for time to enjoy the best parts of life and the best parts of their work.

Research supports the claim that the work can be overwhelming. "According to the National Center for Education Statistics (NCES), 8% of teachers leave the profession yearly and another 8% move to other schools, bringing the total annual turnover rate to 16%. That means that on average, a school will lose 3 out of every 20 teachers" (Wang, 2019, para. 18).

The same concerns apply to education leaders. With the ever-increasing responsibilities of the school principal, for instance, it should be no surprise that in 2012, the Center for Public Education found that the average principal stays on the job for five years or fewer (Hull, 2012).

Self-Evaluation

When was the last time you had a heart-to-heart conversation about your own need for self-care? How would you respond to these three statements as you reflect on your current situation?

1. I find myself dedicating the majority of my work to areas that reflect my strengths and give me the greatest joy in work.

   A. Strongly Agree B. Agree C. Sometimes D. Disagree E. Strongly Disagree

2. Because I invest in my personal growth mentally, physically, spiritually, socially, and financially, I find as much fulfillment in my work as I do in my life outside of work.

   A. Strongly Agree B. Agree C. Sometimes D. Disagree E. Strongly Disagree

3. If money or compensation were no longer necessary, I would still want to do the work I'm currently doing.

   A. Strongly Agree B. Agree C. Sometimes D. Disagree E. Strongly Disagree

Let me encourage you to take inventory of your self-care. The people you serve deserve someone who is taking care of himself or herself. Some ways to do this are by considering your actions, applying the truths learned, and cultivating the most productive habits toward serving others. If you're going to help others, you must learn to first put on your own oxygen mask. Consider these areas of your life:

10 Self-Reflection Areas for Breathing First

1. Learning—Describe your own growth in remaining a lifelong learner. Would you describe your mindset as attentive? Are you regularly reading? How are you developing your ideas and understanding of others and the world? What conferences or training are you attending? How are you allowing deep, rich conversations to shape your understanding? In what ways are engaging in experiences to help broaden your knowledge?

2. Body— Honestly assess your commitment to good nutrition. How often are you engaging in active exercise? How would you describe your sleep patterns? Would you describe your habits as tending excessive or moderate? What commitments have you made to regular breaks or rest? In what ways are you experiencing inspiration? Are you allowing yourself creative or refreshing moments?

3. Influence— Explain how you are intentionally mentoring or coaching someone else. When is the last time you engaged in a purposeful act of service? How do you transfer teaching to moments outside the classroom? What ways are you lifting others by leading them from lessons you have learned? How are you using your unique platform to promote positive change or growth in others?

4. Time— If you conducted an audit of your time, what areas of your day may be ones that could be reprioritized? What boundaries have you set between work and your home life? If someone saw your schedule, where would they say you commit most of your time? What tools are you using to better prioritize your time?

5. Friendships— Name someone in your life you invite to hold you accountable. What supports do you have that provide you honest feedback? Whom do you trust for honest reflection and "just being there" during difficult times? Name one person you invite to consistently challenge your growth and improvement?

6. Spirituality— What role does faith and trust play in your personal growth? Describe how viewing education as a calling may provide more meaning to your work. What benefits may a community of faith or loving support provide you? How do you maintain a long-term perspective on work that so often requires immediate attention?

7. Resources— If your checkbook or bank account was available for review, what may it say about your priorities? How has concern over personal finance influenced your positions or responsibilities in the work you have chosen? If you were completely free from financial worry, how would it affect your short-term and long-term goals as an educator?

8. Intimacy— How are you protecting your most intimate relationships? What role does beauty and wonder play in your life? What milestones are you celebrating along the way? How are you processing the most joyful and sorrowful experiences with those whom you trust and love?

9. Future— Describe ways you are investing in your students or your own children. Would you describe yourself emotionally present or emotionally absent from them? How does mindfulness play a role in your time with those whom you are nurturing or raising?

10. Legacy— Describe your current and long-term goals. Looking back, who are some important people who may deserve gratitude for the growth and perspective you have in your own life? How has celebration, humor and fun assisted you in building meaningful memories?

Fast-Forward

Seven years after our crucial conversation, my wife and I were ushering our kids into an elevator in Washington, D.C. As the doors opened on the third floor, we stepped into the lobby of a large hotel convention ballroom. I was wearing a tuxedo, and my wife was in an evening dress. The girls were in Sunday dresses, and our six-year-old son was in a tie and vest. They had traveled with me as I was receiving an award from the National Association of Secondary School Principals for being recognized as the State of Oklahoma's Assistant Principal of the Year.

As we spent the next few days touring the city, I remember thinking back to that important conversation years before with my wife. Life had still been busy and overwhelming at times. But I had found a new rhythm to my work, life, and family. I was more than a shell of the man I had once been.

Let's Wrap This Up

I wish I could say that I consistently work on all the important areas required for personal growth. The truth is that over the years, I have grown stronger in some areas while neglecting others. Sometimes my wife and I still have crucial conversations about where I need to reprioritize my time and energy. But as you take time to reflect on—instead of neglect—these areas of personal growth, you can continuously refocus your time to those areas that need improvement.

After twenty-five years in the education profession, I would like to share some of those lessons learned with you. That's why this book is so important. If you want to keep growing in your capacity to influence and serve others, you need time for reflection, learning, and taking action for personal growth. If your goal is to influence others in becoming better, you can't ignore this important safety notice: You need to learn to breathe first.

> If your goal is to influence others in becoming better, you can't ignore this important safety notice: You need to learn to breathe first.

Now It's Your Turn

Of the ten self-reflection areas for breathing first described above, what is one area where you want to see personal growth? What is one area out of the ten that you've already seen significant growth?

CHAPTER 1

Your Body

How Are You
Tending Your Garden?

The Garden: *We often underestimate the influence our physical health plays in our thinking, attitude, and performance. Don't beat yourself up if you need to increase your physical fitness. See your body like a gardener sees a garden: a place that needs tilling, cultivation, and attention to produce healthy outcomes.*

When I was little, I loved to stand in the garden as my grandparents tilled soil and put out spring tomatoes. The scent of freshly tilled dirt, the sun beating down on my back, the brush of the ground with hoes and rakes—all these memories come back to me each spring. My grandparents didn't just garden as a hobby. They grew and would can vegetables to use throughout the whole year. To grow that many vegetables, however, they understood the importance of good soil, the right amount of water, and sufficient sunlight.

I have a question for you about the care you are giving an important garden in your life. How are you currently taking care of your body? If what you reap from a healthy garden requires good soil, seed, and care, how is your body any different if you want strong personal outcomes?

As an educator, you understand a lot about learning styles, school culture, and organizational processes. How much do you think your physical health plays into the outcomes happening at your school environment?

In 2009, the U.S. Department of Health and Human Services shared findings that student physical activity contributes to strong academic performance. Here were just three takeaways from the findings:

- Physical activity can help youth improve their concentration, memory, and classroom behavior.
- Youth who spend more time in physical education class do not have lower test scores than youth who spend less time in physical education class.
- Elementary school girls who participated in more physical education had better math and reading tests scores than girls who had less time in physical education ("Youth Physical Activities: The Role of Schools," 2009).

As we encourage our young people to consider the effects of physical activity on their own learning, when was the last time you reflected on how your personal health may be affecting your service to others?

I'm Going to Die!

Over the years, I have learned some hard lessons about neglecting my physical health. One day, I was standing in a meeting with a group of educators from across my district. I was the newest member of the team and the youngest one in a room of fellow educators. As we were waiting for the meeting to begin, every person began sharing about the physical conditions they were currently battling. Each person was taking a different medication for his or her ailments. Everyone shared concerns about cholesterol and heart conditions. As I looked around the room, I began to panic, and I thought, "If I stay in education, I'm going to die!"

Of course, I know every job is stressful and, eventually, we're all going to die. But as I began to seriously reflect on my experience as a young education leader, I realized I had gained twenty pounds. I skipped meals or ate convenience food because school activities were more important than good nutrition. I had stopped exercising because I needed the extra time to catch up on emails or other school projects. Frankly, I was a mess and felt like it most of the time. I knew I had to make time for healthier fitness and nutrition habits. And as I did, I began to notice a difference in the way I worked. A commitment to better health, nutrition, and exercise began to give me more energy, focus, and creativity.

5 Tips for Caring for Your Body

Let me share five ways I have invested in personal health, not as a prescription, just as an example of how one educator has learned to adopt healthier choices into his busy days.

1. Yes, exercise.
I have a three-mile route I like to run in my neighborhood. For years, I tried to schedule time at the gym or exercise after school, but it just didn't work for me. So, when I decided to begin exercising, I bought a pair of running shoes. Instead of waking up early to check emails, I woke up early to run. It was the easiest choice for me. I'd just put on my shoes, stretch, and run, and it was all over in thirty minutes. Even though it has taken me years to develop this habit, it is one of the most important habits for my physical and mental health. I have solved a lot of major problems and conflicts during those runs. I've prayed a lot during those

runs. And I've come to see things from the perspective of my wife and others during those runs.

Why is exercise so good for you? It's great for your cardio-vascular health. Just like your car needs an oil change, your body needs oxygen flowing through every one of its cells. Also, when you engage in prolonged physical activity, your body produces an endorphin release—a natural high that increases your energy and even makes exercise something you can enjoy.

2. Eat your veggies.

I love food. In fact, when I was growing up, my mom always kept an extra-large bowl in the kitchen just for me. When we'd have chili, for instance, she always put mine in the largest bowl because she knew I'd want seconds or thirds. I was always active as a kid, so eating a lot didn't seem to be a problem. But as I began work in education, I was a lot less active.

In addition to exercise, I also had to make better nutritional choices. Most mornings, I'll start the day with oatmeal and a cup of coffee. Lunches are usually something light — a sandwich and fruit. My biggest meals are normally in the evenings and best when we can enjoy them as a family. The older I get, the less meat I am eating.

Let's be clear. If you decide to fill up on potato chips and soda, then your body will have to digest trans fats and sugar. You'll have less energy. Your heart will have to work harder, not smarter. And your brain will have reacted to the intake by a peak in energy followed by a plunge in energy. Frankly, I'm not eating nearly as nutritiously as I need to be, but little habits create long-term results. As a result of better choices, I've been able to keep off extra pounds and my cholesterol levels have been good. Here's another little secret I practice: Whenever someone delivers doughnuts or cake to the school, instead of giving in to the temptation, I'll take one and allow myself one bite and throw the rest of my piece away. I can honestly tell someone thanks for sharing the delicious treat with me, but I also just saved my body hundreds of unnecessary calories to burn.

3. Hit the pillow.

I like to combine sleep and rest into one category because they are connected. If you don't set a time each night to unplug from technology and wind down, you will have a hard time sleeping. Yes, there are times when deadlines or activities push you into late hours. But you must create a habit of winding down. For the most part, I start my wind-down time around 9:00 each night so I can be asleep before 10:00 and wake up by 5:00 or 5:30 each morning.

Also, I make a commitment not to work on Sundays. I know Sundays are historically days of rest for many people of faith. I used to think not working was silly until I realized I was staying engaged in school activities (grading papers, catching up on emails) seven days a week. When I began to protect Sunday as a day to worship, to rest, and to be with family, I found myself better able to finish important projects before Sunday. Try it, and I believe you'll find more creativity after giving yourself a whole day of break from work projects.

4. Say no to excess and yes to moderation.

I'm going to be blunt here. If you enjoy alcohol, coffee, sweets, or meat, do so in moderation. First, you will feel better when you do. Second, you will most likely behave better too. If you're like me, you don't enjoy being around others when their intake of anything becomes an unhealthy obsession. And yes, the area where I struggle most is definitely with coffee—and I'm still working on it.

5. Seek inspiration.

If you think about how your body is designed for movement, it only makes sense that if you are engaged in heart-pumping, endorphin-releasing activities, your mindset and your brain benefit as a result. When you take time for good nutrition and rest, you will begin to think more clearly, and that is when creativity and inspiration have room to grow. For some people, being active means a long hike or walk. For others, it is dancing. For some of my friends, it means hunting and fishing. Whatever activity it takes, make time each day to practice good habits for your body so you can enjoy the benefits that occur as a result. Your mind is better conditioned for sharp thinking when your body is experiencing good health.

> Your mind is better conditioned for sharp thinking when your body is experiencing good health.

Let's Wrap This Up

Recently, I gathered some fresh lettuce from a raised bed in my backyard, which my wife and I shared for lunch. The vegetables we grow are not nearly as bountiful as my grandparents' gardens. But the same truths apply to both: Good soil, lots of water, and sufficient sunlight can yield yummy produce.

I don't know where you are in your journey. You may already be active and making healthy choices. Or you may be discouraged and battling health challenges. Whatever your situation, be encouraged to take whatever steps work for you. And know that each positive step you take creates movement toward healthier results.

Now It's Your Turn

Here are some questions for self-reflection:

1. How is my nutrition—what goes into my body—affecting my concentration and energy?
2. How is my physical activity—or lack of it—influencing the way I feel about tackling big projects?
3. Am I allowing sleep and rest to influence my levels of patience and endurance?
4. In what ways am I letting moderation—or lack of it— affect my habits or relationships?
5. Does my overall physical health lead to more inspiration or tend toward more anxiety?
6. Now, what is one step I can take this week toward healthier choices?

The way you treat yourself will affect the way you treat others. So, do yourself and others a favor, and keep taking care of your body. As you do, you will find more energy and creativity for doing what matters.

CHAPTER 2

Your Mind

What's On Your Mental Playlist?

***

The Playlist: *It's simple but true: What you take into your mind and rehearse in your thoughts will influence your ideas and actions. Think of your brain as a playlist. What are you consistently putting in? How does that affect the way you influence others?*

My mother-in-law has Alzheimer's. The condition began about ten years ago when we thought she was simply becoming more forgetful. But as her short-term memory declined, we realized she wasn't just suffering from old age. Over the years, she has lost the ability to recognize her own children and grandchildren, and she forgets whether or not her parents are still living—even though they passed away more than thirty years ago. This is what Alzheimer's can do to the brain.

Music and the Brain

On Sunday afternoons, we like to take our children to visit Grandma at the memory care center where she now lives. We keep an electronic piano in her room because she loves playing and singing hymns. When I visit, I sit at the keys and open a hymnal. As soon as my fingers play a chord, Grandma joins in and doesn't miss a beat. She remembers the tunes and words of all her favorite songs. We will sing one song and then another.

I'm not a neuroscientist, but I have studied learning styles and child development. Memorization is often easiest when combined with music. It works for children, adults, and apparently for my mother-in-law with Alzheimer's too (Sauer, 2014). According to research reported by CNN's Elizabeth Landau in 2012, it is also good practice for brain engagement (Landau, 2012).

My Daughter's Playlist

Occasionally, my daughter Katie and I will drive together to see Grandma. Katie is a senior in high school, and she has some great playlists on her iPhone. She tags them with different titles, but one she calls "Dad's Playlist." It is a compilation of mostly acoustic or musical numbers. On our drives over, we turn up the volume in my car and sing along. One of my favorite duets is from *The Greatest Showman*— "Rewrite the Stars" with Zac Efron and Zendaya singing.

> *What if we rewrite the stars?*
> *Say you were made to be mine*
> *Nothing could keep us apart*
> *You'd be the one I was meant to find...*

As fun as it is to connect with my family through music, I would like to ask you a question about your own playlist— and I don't just mean the songs or music you enjoy. What is on your mental playlist?

Our brains are powerful organs. And just as digesting nutritious food promotes better health, what you digest in your mind shapes your view of yourself and the world around you and forms life-long habits and memories. In a world of constant access to technology, advertisements, news, and information, our brains encounter stimuli at alarming rates.

In an article based on his book, *The Organized Mind: Thinking Straight in the Age of Information Overload,* Daniel J. Levitin, shares the following:

Information scientists have quantified [that in] 2011, Americans took in five times as much information every day as they did in 1986— the equivalent of 174 newspapers. During our leisure time, not counting work, each of us processes 34 gigabytes, or 100,000 words, every day. The world's 21,274 television stations produce 85,000 hours of original programming every day as we watch an average of five hours of television daily, the equivalent of 20 gigabytes of audio-video images. That's not counting YouTube, which uploads 6,000 hours of video every hour. And computer gaming? It consumes more bytes than all other media put together, including DVDs, TV, books, magazines, and the Internet (Levitin, 2015, para. 3).

So how do you ensure that what you "ingest" with your brain is as healthy as what you digest with your body? Frankly, if you want to keep growing in your critical thinking and reasoning, you must be proactive about what's on your mental playlist. As I've shared before, my suggestions are not prescriptive. But here are some suggestions from one veteran educator to others:

Five Areas to Reflect on as You Regulate Your Information Intake

1. How is your mindset?

A lot of educational research has been shared in recent years about the power of cultivating and maintaining a learning mindset. In 2007, Carol Dweck shared some powerful takeaways in her book *Mindset: The New Psychology of Success*. She discussed how the ways we approach learning influence the ways we learn (Dweck, 2007).

Your frame-of-mind and willingness to learn are important. Resisting change, refusing to innovate, and looking at obstacles and giving up are recipes for lack of growth. Not only do we need to encourage environments of risk-taking and experimentation for our students and teachers, but we also need to practice those habits ourselves. One way to do this is by simply being mindful throughout each day.

Mindset and *mindfulness* have become buzz words as of late. But mindfulness really is an important way for many people to guide their thoughts, practice meditation, or increase stress-relief. And although these are healthy practices, when I talk about being mindful, I'm simply talking about being aware of the present and being purposeful in engaging with your environment. I don't do this all the time, but let me give you an example:

When you are spending time in a classroom or observing students, instead of simply relying on a rubric or lesson plan, take the first few minutes to simply be mindful. Look around your environment. Stare into the faces of the children and watch whether they are engaged. Be aware of your interactions with others, even in the small moments. Are you treating others with concern and interest or acting as if they don't exist? Are you asking clarifying questions so that you understand what is really happening? Being mindful keeps you aware that each moment can be one of learning or understanding.

This applies inside and outside of the classroom. The other day, I was driving on a highway when I saw a railroad bridge suspended above the road. A freight train was speeding across it. As I approached, I realized the amazing moment I was about to experience. I was sitting in a 2,000-pound steel and aluminum wrapped machine, rolling forward through the use of a combustible engine, encased by intricately engineered parts, and carried by four rubber tires. As I was gliding across an asphalt road, I would soon pass under a metal bridge holding the weight of several freight cars, each possibly weighing over 200,000 pounds.

What would my great-grandfather have thought of that moment? He had come to Oklahoma on a cattle run in the early 1900s and met my grandmother at the boarding house of a Baptist minister. When he married the minister's daughter, they returned to Tennessee in a horse-drawn wagon. Could he have ever imagined traveling sixty-five miles per hour in an automobile while simultaneously passing under a speeding freight train?

> Your mindset plays a powerful role in your openness to continual learning.

Why share this example of being mindful? Besides admitting I'm a bit weird, at that moment I was choosing to acknowledge realities and perspectives that are so easy to ignore in the fast-paced, modern world in which we live. Being aware of your surroundings allows you to take in the moment, appreciate its meaning, and experience more than simply going from point A to point B. Your mindset plays a powerful role in your openness to continual learning.

2. What are you reading?

If you look at my nightstand or on my iPhone, you'll find books I enjoy. Just this past week, I finished re-reading *The Fellowship of the Ring* by

J.R.R. Tolkien, and I listened to the audiobook *The Wright Brothers* by David McCullough. Stories about others, like the Wright brothers, can inspire you to think about the hard work required for innovation and exploration (McCullough, 2015). In what ways are you purposefully engaging your mind through what you read?

Although I enjoy reading and listening to educational books, I also try to keep a fictional book, historical fiction, or biography on hand. Stories provide a wealth of information about the experiences others have encountered. Reading allows you to take a deeper dive into someone else's mind. Often someone else's perspective or logic gives you a new or deeper understanding of the human experience.

Although my practice is only one example, I have a morning routine that includes reading a passage from the Bible, and I usually digest some audio content on my commute to work. Later, I may take in the news or a podcast on my drive home. And at night, I try to read a book of fiction or an historical narrative.

Over the years, my life has been influenced by the valuable lessons I've found in books. I've listened to the wisdom of heroes like George Washington and Fredrick Douglas. I've experienced new cultures from brave souls like Amy Tan and Chinua Achebe. I've survived death camps with legends like Corrie Ten Boon and Louis Zamperini. I've cried and laughed with Kathryn Stockett and grieved and lamented with George Orwell. Whatever your favorite genre, books are a great way to enter the minds and lives of others and potentially have your thoughts changed as a result.

3. How are you growing professionally?

As important as it is to expand your mind through great literature, you also must grow by encountering other strong educators. For years, I felt guilty when I had the opportunity to attend a workshop, conference, or engage in great professional development. Yes, I sat through some required professional development sessions with mixed results;

some trainings were more helpful than others. But as I was able to learn about topics that immediately influenced my work, I found learning from others a powerful way of experiencing professional growth. I think part of my "feeling guilty" came from an unidentified belief that self-improvement was somehow selfish. Over time, however, I have come to realize that as you

> as you grow in your own professional knowledge and skill set, you also increase your capacity to help others grow

grow in your own professional knowledge and skill set, you also increase your capacity to help others grow—a very unselfish application to personal and professional growth.

In addition to face-to-face learning, technology now provides access to a world of information via podcasts, webinars, and videos. Make a commitment to engage with topics relating to the areas you currently teach or lead. Find great professional development like Solution Tree's Professional Learning Communities Conferences. Or subscribe to podcasts by educators like *10 Minute Teacher Podcast* (Davis, 2020), *StartEdUpInnovation Podcast* (Wettrick, 2020), or podcasts by educational leadership experts like *Principal Center Radio* (Baeder, 2019), *Transformative Principal Podcast* (Jones, 2019*), Better Leaders, Better Schools Podcast* (Bauer, 2019), or my own: *Principal Matters Podcast* (Parker, 2019).

Also, consider these other ways to engage in powerful professional learning, which will expand your thinking:

- Tour a neighboring classroom or school and compare the practices of other educators with your own.
- Talk to colleagues about the ways they've solved problems similar to the ones you are currently encountering.

- Attend workshops for professional development.
- Listen to a podcast or webinar series.

4. How are you valuing your experiences?

All good teachers know that experience is an amazing instructor. But we often fail to learn deeply when we fail to reflect on our experiences. When I began blogging seven years ago, it was a way to journal and catalog ideas, steps, and lessons learned from my experience as a school administrator. Each time you encounter a situation, you gain the privilege of experience to gauge what is and is not working well.

A few years ago, these ideas became clear to me when I attended a workshop with author Pete Hall on the *Continuum of Self-Reflection*. Pete taught that you have a natural process in the way you experience learning, which allows you continuous growth if you practice awareness of your experiences, reflecting on your successes or failures, taking action based on those lessons learned, and then refining your practice based on those cycles of learning (Hall and Simeral, 2008).

Yes, you can grow your capacity for learning by digesting information from others' experiences. But your own experience provides a powerful way to assess, measure, refine, and apply lessons as you continue to grow in your practice. As Malcolm Gladwell revealed in his book *Outliers: The Story of Success,* people tend to master skill with 10,000 hours of engagement and practice. Even as you experience the ups and downs of educational practice, you are moving closer to mastery in some areas while still growing in others (Gladwell, 2013).

Let's Wrap This Up

I find a lot of joy in knowing that I can connect with my daughter or mother-in-law through their unique playlists. I sometimes wonder what memories or thoughts will be deeply embedded in my mind as I grow older. None of us have the guarantee of healthy brains as we age. But we do have a choice over the kind of information, thoughts, stories, music, and ideas we think about today. And as you purposely influence your thoughts by being mindful, digesting great books, enjoying professional development, and reflecting on experiences, you are adding to your own playlist of ideas to live by. And you increase your ability to positively influence others.

Now It's Your Turn

We all enjoy learning from those who stay fresh in their own intellectual growth. As you take the next step of investing in your own thinking, others will benefit from your awareness, lessons, and experiences too. In what ways are you purposefully seeking out heathy practices for your thinking? How can you be more mindful of the people, places, and situations you will encounter this week? What books will you read next for your personal growth? How can you take advantage of workshops or professional development? What ways can you practice cycles of reflection on your practices and experiences?

CHAPTER 3

Your Influence

Is Your Input Producing Healthy or Toxic Environments?

Pollution: *None of us want to live in a place with polluted air. It's bad for our health and the long-term quality of life for everyone around us. Is your influence on others toxic or refreshing?*

In 2010, I had the privilege of traveling to China for ten days on an educational tour. One morning in Beijing, I left the hotel before breakfast for a quick run. Later, as I showered and dressed, I began to feel sick. I thought perhaps I was catching a cold or just suffering from jet lag. Over the next few days, we visited Tiananmen Square, the Forbidden City, and the Great Wall before traveling to another city.

As we toured Beijing, I noticed the skies were never blue. But on our trips outside of the city, the skies were clear. When I mentioned my observation to our tour guide, he told us it had been an especially cloudy season that summer in the city. But when we left Beijing a few days later, the skies cleared again.

I'm sure you have heard of China's rising problems with smog and pollution as many of its cities modernized, but I soon realized firsthand why I felt sick when I went running. Thankfully, since my trip there, China has begun addressing many of these concerns as health risks became a public concern. When was the last time you thought about the air you breathe? Not just the physical oxygen you breathe in, but the emotional, cultural, and relational atmospheres that surround you? More importantly, what kind of atmosphere are you creating for those whom you are leading? Are you helping create an environment of clean, healthy intakes, or are you contributing to an atmosphere of cultural pollution?

These are important questions to reflect on as educators because every school or organization has a culture. And that culture significantly affects the outcomes you will produce. Spend time in any school or with any team and you'll soon get a feeling for the positive and negative influences happening there.

Both teachers and principals play essential roles when it comes to influencing school culture. In 2011, The Wallace Foundation, along with the National Association of Elementary School Principals (NAESP) and the National Association of Secondary School Principals (NASSP), shared research showing how principal leadership ranked second only to the quality of teachers in significantly affecting school outcomes (Wallace Foundation, 2011).

According to the research findings, principals influence schools in five specific ways:

1. Shaping a vision of academic success based on high standards for all students.

2. Creating a climate hospitable to education so that safety, a cooperative spirit, and other foundations of fruitful interaction prevail.
3. Cultivating leadership so that teachers and adults assume their roles in realizing the school's vision.
4. Improving instruction to enable teachers to teach at their best and students to learn at their utmost.
5. Managing people, data, and processes to foster school improvement (NAESP/NAESP Joint Report, 2013).

Teachers and administrators influence student outcomes. Your influence matters. In light of the research and practices that inform student outcomes, I want to suggest five ways you can examine the kind of influence you are having—the kind of air you're providing for others to breathe at your school.

5 Takeaways for Increasing Your Positive Influence

1. Be a mentor.

I'll never forget my first assignment as an assistant principal. The very first day of school, we encountered a student in possession of drugs on campus. Another assistant principal in my building at the time was Lydia Wilson. Not only did Lydia model how to interact with students and parents, but she also used every opportunity to teach me basic skills—like how to conduct a lawful search, how to correctly document meetings, and how to appropriately follow through with disciplinary action and educational supports. Lydia was my mentor, and her influence gave me the confidence to manage future disciplinary incidents on my own.

Over the years, I've had other great mentors as a teacher and administrator, but I also had mentors in the years before stepping into the education profession. My college professors, internship supervisors, and veteran educators would coach me through observations, over lunches, or just be available when I had questions. My mentors helped me navigate how to manage difficult situations with students or build partnerships with parents. Hopefully, you've had similar experiences. I like to think that by mentoring others, I'm helping pay forward the debt of gratitude I owe my mentors. You have the same privilege. Whether you are working with teachers, administrators, or students, you can model and reflect with those around you.

Just this past week, I had a first-year assistant principal, Chris Berg, from South Bend, Indiana, reach out to me via Twitter. He messaged me the following: "PMP (Principal Matters Podcast) has meant so much to me this year. I felt like I had my own personal mentor helping me adjust to becoming an administrator." I could not have been more encouraged when I read those words. What lessons are you learning and passing along to others? How are you are creating healthy mental and emotional air for them? Make the choice to see your relationships with others as an opportunity to mentor.

Educators often feel isolated in in their roles in classrooms or while leading others. If you are simply managing, organizing, and facilitating the necessary functions of your school, you may be missing out on an opportunity to grow other leaders in the process. Mentorship is one way to keep a strong influence on others and share the lessons you're learning.

2. Be a servant leader.
Let's face it. If you took the position of an educator as an easy job assignment, you have already discovered you made the wrong choice. However, if your goal is to provide a better learning environment for all the students and members of the school community you serve, you know the importance of getting your hands dirty in the process—sometimes literally.

In addition to being willing to put in the necessary work for planning lessons, building schedules, providing resources, and scheduling meetings, sometimes you may need to pick up trash, paint walls, mop up spills, or weed flower beds—whatever is required to provide the kind of school environment you would want for your own children. Being a servant leader does not mean you give up your primary responsibilities to do someone else's job. It means that you are willing to pitch in whenever needed. And sometimes you step in so that people see you are willing to perform the tasks you're asking others to perform or manage.

> Being a servant leader does not mean you give up your primary responsibilities to do someone else's job. It means that you are willing to pitch in whenever needed.

Superintendent, Rick Thomas, began his position in my last district by modeling servant leadership. His first day of work, he did not show up in a suit and tie. Instead, he wore work clothes and brought a weed eater with him. The year before, our former superintendent had been indicted for embezzling school funds. It was a challenging time, and our community had lost a great deal of trust in our district's leadership. In the process, many areas had been neglected, including some of the groundwork on our campuses. Rick Thomas felt it was necessary to immediately address this need. When he began trimming and beautifying campuses, the parents, teachers, and district staff who saw him working that day took lots of photos and shared them on social media. And Mr. Thomas immediately set the tone for his first year by modeling the way. Everyone was expected to do whatever it took to serve students—starting with him.

3. Lead by example.

I know this seems like a no-brainer, but all educators are leaders, and sometimes leaders need to be reminded to simply lead. In fact, I once heard an experienced educator say, "Whenever I'm unsure of the decision I need to make in a hard situation, I will ask myself, 'What would a great leader do in this situation?' and act accordingly." Education is often a lonely endeavor. You are faced with difficult options and scenarios. You are asked to make bold and courageous choices that no one else but you needs to make.

One of my earliest mentors told me to always keep in mind three things: Be Fair, Be Firm, and Be Consistent. In his bestseller *Good to Great: Why Some Companies Make the Leap and Others Don't*, Jim Collins describes the most successful companies in America. One compelling similarity among them was strong leadership—not the kind you see in flashy politicians or celebrities, but the consistent, hardworking, calculated, and focused leadership necessary to move entire organizations toward achievement (Collins, 2001).

Being decisive means thinking about how your decisions affect others with justice and equity. It means reaching out to trusted colleagues if you need wise feedback. It means taking action and being consistent in your own decisions so your students and fellow educators have stability and support in the work they perform.

You've probably heard that leadership is like pulling a rope. You cannot move a rope by pushing it; you move it most easily by pulling it along with you. When you are responsible for others, you must learn to lead them with confident guidance. You're much more effective if you go first and bring others along with you rather than tell them or push them toward your shared goals.

4. Keep teaching.

Educators use every opportunity to teach others helpful lessons for their growth. Whether you are meeting with a student about grades, managing a parent conference, or strategizing with a professional learning team, how can you take advantage of every moment to convey new or helpful knowledge?

You must model the kind of right brain and left brain approaches you know also work with students. If you are a principal, for example, take advantage of visiting classrooms to communicate goals with students, and don't be afraid to model some lessons. Run your professional development meetings and faculty meetings the way you would want a great classroom to operate. If you are teacher, don't forget that building relationships with parents is as powerful as building relationships with their children. Even as you manage accountability with others, ask yourself how you can use those moments as teachable ones. Take advantage of every moment to still be a teacher.

This also means you don't avoid having crucial conversations or hesitate from confronting stark realities in your classroom or at your school. However, when you do, you do so with the kind of care and concern you would want someone using with you.

> If you are teacher, don't forget that building relationships with parents is as powerful as building relationships with their children.

Over the course of my career as an educator, I would frequently talk to students about their interests or pursuits. Sometimes I would give them ideas or lessons on how to maximize their opportunities. A few months ago, one of my former students, Lily Cummings, sent a message to the teachers at my former high school via Facebook. In the message of thanks to our staff and teachers, she also included this note to me: *To Mr. Parker whom I consider myself so lucky to have had as a principal. He kept the school's spirit alive and always encouraged me to start a blog and do more. He even accompanied me by playing piano as I sang at senior assembly (Cummings, 2017).*

Little notes like this remind me that you can never overestimate the impact or influence you may be having on others through offering teachable moments.

5. Build platforms.

The last way I suggest you increase your positive influence is by examining how you are sharing ideas and guidance beyond even your own classroom, school, or team. How are you passing along the lessons, takeaways, and golden-nuggets of your education experiences with a wider audience?

Seven years ago, I began blogging about my experiences in education. At first, it was in response to a lot of questions I was receiving from new or aspiring leaders. Later, I began to realize how social media, blogging, and podcasting were powerful platforms. Often, when I have an idea that I need to communicate, I find an outlet through my blog and podcast creation. I'm not suggesting you must use the same platforms to positively influence others (although I think it would be cool if you did), but I am suggesting that you find a medium to communicate your expertise and experience to others who are in a professional role of education. They deserve to know and learn from your experience, and frankly, you cannot afford to be selfish with your knowledge.

We are always stronger collectively than individually. Whether contributing an article to a school newsletter, speaking as a guest at to a college education class, presenting at a conference, or starting your own YouTube channel—think of ways you can be a voice of experience and reflection for others in your profession. Don't keep your influence limited to just your immediate audience. Build platforms for sharing your ideas with those who could benefit from your lessons.

Let's Wrap This Up

Author and motivational speaker Jon Gordon has a term for people who negatively influence others. He calls them "energy vampires" (Gordon, 2015). You know what I'm talking about, right? Every school and organization has team members who tend to suck the positivity out of conversations or meetings.

When was the last time you asked yourself how you are affecting the emotional and cultural air that others breathe? Are you being an energy builder or an energy vampire? As you lead your students or your school community, keep in mind the power of your influence. And make it a goal to help others breathe easier through your mentoring, serving, leading, teaching, and platform building.

Now It's Your Turn

What kind of atmosphere are your teachers, students, and others encountering when they enter your classroom or your school? What is one way you can positively influence the students, parents, or colleagues around you today? As you know, education is a calling, not just a career. And your ability to serve depends greatly on your ability to see the power of your influence. The way you lead others will influence whether those around you are breathing in healthy or toxic emotional oxygen.

CHAPTER 4

Your Time

Are You Making the
Most of Each Moment?

The Count-Down: *Time is a measured and relative quantity. And each of us receives the same amount each day. Your life is also limited by time. How can you make each moment more meaningful?*

*B*alance is a popular word among life coaches and leadership authors. As important as it is to invest in the meaningful areas of your life, too many people place unrealistic expectations upon themselves. Living a life of meaning does not mean being perfect. This misperception is not only unrealistic, it is also unhealthy. Life is messy. Sometimes you face unexpected challenges in your health, relationships, or finances. When you look at your own condition, no matter how exhilarating or depressing, the first response should be to give yourself the kind of grace you would want to extend to someone you love. We all face ups and downs.

But sometimes we need reminders to refocus on what matters. It's a delicate but important tension to be aware of both truths:

1. You need to invest in what matters to keep growing.
2. You need to be patient with yourself (and others) along the journey.

I'd like to add some thoughts for educators about how to better manage your time, but I want to offer these as suggestions, not prescriptions. You do not need any more guilt than you likely already have about the difficulty of balancing your responsibilities. But you may gain some valuable ideas in the following discussion about time.

What Are Your Goals for Your Time?

Several years ago, I was talking to a friend of mine who is twenty years younger than I. He and his wife were establishing life after college. They had just become parents, and his small business was beginning to grow. I was reflecting with him about my own memories at his age: how my wife and I had lived on one income to pay off college debts with our second income and how we had saved up to buy our first home before our first baby was born.

As I celebrated his journey and reminisced about my own, he asked an honest but thought-provoking question: "So, what goals have you set for yourself now?"

I paused for a moment and then answered as honestly as I could. "Well," I said, "I think my biggest goal right now is to simply survive!"

With a growing family and the demands of being an assistant principal at the time, I couldn't think of a better answer. It was honest, but over the next several days, those words haunted me. When was the last time I had really thought about the next goals I wanted to reach for myself or my family?

During that same time, I came across a podcast interview with Robert Smith, author of *20,000 Days and Counting: The Crash Course for Mastering Your Life Right Now*. Robert relayed how at age fifty-five, he realized he had lived 20,000 days (Smith, 2013). When you look at life from that perspective, you realize that if you are blessed with a life of 75 years, you have approximately 27,375 days to live. On my next birthday, I will be fifty-two years old, which means I will have reached 18,980 days. If I make it to 75 years old, that means I have approximately 8,300 days to go!

You may be doing the math in your own head now. No matter where you are on the scale, you realize that we all have a limited number of days, hours, and minutes remaining. We can either make the most of them, or we can look back with regret on the moments lost. Without overwhelming you with the guilt that comes from trying to achieve perfect balance, I want to encourage you to think about how to make the most of your time so you still take calculated risks and have fewer regrets. None of us ever does this perfectly, but when we begin to have perspective of our time, we can begin to set sensible goals.

Many educators struggle mightily with managing time. Principals, for example, struggle with the demands of their job descriptions. Researchers from the Center for Education Policy Analysis shared findings in a helpful report, *Principal Time Management Skills: Explaining Patterns in Principals' Time Use and Effectiveness*. In the report, Jason A. Grissom (Vanderbilt University), Susanna Loeb (Stanford University), and Hajime Mitani (Stanford University), shared that time management among principals is a strategy for "increasing their focus on instructional leadership and pursuing school improvement," (Grissom, Jason, et al, 2015, para. 1). Teachers and administrators alike are better able to serve students and school communities when they are well-planned, organized, punctual, and responsible with their time.

So, how can you approach your need for time management and goal setting so that you are making the most of the days you have set before you?

6 Tips for Making the Most of Your Time

1. Reduce time-wasting activities.
One of the biggest ways you find your time mismanaged is by allowing others or circumstances to dictate its use. At the risk of sounding like your grandfather, let me caution you about some time wasters to avoid:

- Social Media
  It is a time-sucker. If you check it during the day, set a time limit; otherwise, you can find precious minutes wasted randomly scrolling through photos, feeds, and chats. Although social media can be a good way to stay connected to professional learning or build important friendships, do not allow it to become a distraction or create unnecessary anxiety for you.

- Screen Time
  Whether it is TV, your computer, or your smartphone, if you are spending more time in front of a screens than interacting with people, you are most likely not building relationships. You'll never hear people on their death beds say they wish they had spent more time online.

- Emails
  Set a timer for 10-15 minutes and read as many emails as you can. Respond to the ones that require only a quick response. For those that require more thought, follow-up later. Tag them accordingly or delegate them to an appropriate team member for follow-up if the question is outside your area of responsibility. Keep your calendar handy as many emails require meetings and dates. If an email reveals heightened emotions, call that person or see someone face-to-face when possible. Move to other to-dos after your time is up.

- Driving or Commuting

  Take advantage of this time to learn, either by catching up on news, sports, or listening to podcasts or audio books. If you love to sing, use this time to let it rip. By all means, don't take out frustrations by distracted or angry driving.

- School Events or Activities

  If you have a choice, don't feel pressured to stay till the end of every event—especially if another trustworthy and authorized adult is present to manage the activity. Take advantage of these "down times" for other tasks or to-dos. People often ask me how I found time to write and be a principal. The answer is that I learned to combine tasks. For years, I carried my laptop to away games. Especially during tournaments, I would take advantage of the times between games to do some writing—a hobby I enjoyed and an activity that allowed me to write my first two books.

2. Set sensible boundaries.

I'm going to keep this point short. You can say no to requests. I know it's hard, but if you have taken the time to schedule what matters in advance (I'll talk about that next), then you should already know in advance what your time is committed to. It's also important to ask others to help you set boundaries.

Let me share an example as a former principal. In my school's office area, I asked my secretary to protect the time of my teachers and me. I modeled scenarios for her that we practiced together. If parents called, she knew what questions to ask to see whether or not the call should be forwarded to a teacher, counselor, or to me. Most often, the person they needed to talk to was someone on my team more directly involved in the outcomes of their students. Setting boundaries on whom I needed to speak to or call back saved me hours of time each week. This same rule applies every day. As hard as it can be, learn to politely say no when your plate is already too full to add more.

3. Schedule what matters.

You probably already keep a detailed calendar. I suggest that educators set their calendars at least a year in advance. Sometimes, two-year calendars are helpful for major meeting dates like start dates, annual events, and graduation ceremonies. For instance, during my summers as a principal, I would divide my teachers into groups and decide whose classrooms I would spend time in each week for formal observations. I still conducted daily or weekly walkthroughs throughout the entire campus, but each week, two or three teachers knew in advance that I would be spending an entire classroom period with them.

By setting these teacher observations on my calendar in advance for the targeted week, I could reach out to them the week before to coordinate the best day and period for a visit. Because I had already prioritized whose classrooms I would be observing throughout the entire school year, I could fit all my other meetings around those classroom visits.

The same strategy works for teachers who set their syllabus and curriculum in place for the entire year in advance. In addition to learning goals, teachers know they will be conducting or participating in emergency drills, team meetings, student assemblies, or other professional development meetings. Place learning goals and other scheduled events or meetings on your calendar before the school year begins. Yes, emergency situations often derail even the best-made plans, but you can often keep those moments in perspective when you commit yourself ahead of time to the tasks you know are best for overall student outcomes.

4. Use tools to save time.

A tool can be either digital or physical. I have found both helpful in saving time. First, I suggest you have a physical location for the letters, paperwork, and mail you need to see, sign, or throw out. Normally, I would begin my day going through the mail placed in my box the afternoon before. With each article, I would either trash the unnecessary, respond to inquiries to return by mail, keep what needs filing, or forward on letters or publications to others on my team.

When it comes to digital tools, I love Google Docs and Google Forms. For instance, my school team and I would keep our duty rosters, master schedule, emergency drills, observation schedules, or team meetings on Google Docs so we could share documents among team members and update or edit as needed. These documents are easily updated from year-to-year. Google Forms is also a great way to collect data or survey feedback from multiple sources and place them in an easy-to-read spreadsheet later.

I also suggest sharing a digital calendar with your students or teammates. They can see what is on your calendar in advance and know when you may or may not be available for upcoming meetings. For teachers, this also becomes a consistent way to keep a digital make-up calendar available for students. Use Google Calendars or whatever email service you have to schedule parent meetings and meetings with students.

When I was a high school principal, I would ask my senior students who were speaking at graduation to submit their speeches to me via Google Docs. We would coordinate edits and compare speeches in advance to avoid repetition or limit wording if speeches ran too long. Perhaps you are a fan of Evernote, Outlook, or the To-Do-ist App. Whatever tools you choose, your goal is to coordinate with others to save time.

5. Prioritize and tackle accordingly.

I often hear educators say they are frustrated by being unable to accomplish everything on their to-do list. This is a common reality for anyone with lots of responsibilities. Here is a simple truth: You will always have more on your to-do list than can be accomplished by one person. The goal is to prioritize the competing demands on your time.

That is one reason to set important projects, meetings, and deadlines on your calendar well in advance. Your first priority is student learning.

And you cannot serve as an effective instructor or instructional leader if you're not first prioritizing learning goals with the students and others in your professional learning community. At the same time, you may be the only person responsible for managing a specific assignment, like being a class sponsor. If you are a principal, you may be the one responsible for handling a school-wide crisis or emergency. Keep these competing demands in perspective.

Let me say a few words to education leaders: Principals, often you can "chunk" your tasks. For instance, you may know on a given day that you want to complete two formal observations, work on a report requested by your state department, and manage scheduled meetings with teachers or parents. Just as teachers and students work with scheduled periods, chunk your time as well. If you need to see students from discipline referrals, try to schedule these back-to-back within the first hour of school by having your hall passes written out before school begins and seeing students early in the day so you can resolve issues as soon as possible with parent and teacher follow-up. Position yourself in the hallways during passing periods so you see as many students as possible throughout the day. Walk the building and stop by rooms to say hello or monitor school procedures on your way to formal observations. Schedule a block of time or part of one class period of a day for a meeting with yourself to finish your reports. Hold

> No matter how hard you work as an educator, you will still end your day with many tasks undone, but the goal is to prioritize the tasks that most directly impact the learning, culture, and climate of your classroom and school community.

non-emergency phone calls or email follow-ups for the end of the day when students or teachers have left the building.

Whether you are a teacher or administrator, throughout the entire day, make time to take photos of student achievements and include shout-outs on social media of the great happenings throughout your classrooms and school. No matter how hard you work as an educator, you will still end your day with many tasks undone, but the goal is to prioritize the tasks that most directly impact the learning, culture, and climate of your classroom and school community. When you do, you will keep your school moving in a positive direction.

6. Schedule time for what inspires you.

Recently, I was reading an article on Inc.com by Bryan Adams titled *How Google's 20 Percent Rule Can Make You More Productive and Energetic*. Google's commitment to allowing its employees to use 20% of their time on a creative, Google-related passion project has increased the company's outcomes and improved employee engagement (Adams, 2016). I find this mindset can be especially empowering for educators, too. This may look different for each person, but ask yourself: What is one area of your classroom, school, or team where you want to see improvement? And what is a way you would enjoy working on that outcome that matches your passion or skillset?

Throughout the week, think of creative ways to display student or teacher success through the use of creative social media shares, videos, or blog posts. Pick a topic of importance and write about it in your next classroom or school newsletter.

At the end of an especially hard day, pause and ask the question: What is one step I took today to move the needle one degree in a more positive direction? Then send an encouraging email to a co-worker or post a kudo to a group of teachers or student organizations to encourage them in a positive way. Take a few minutes to just write reflectively on both successes and struggles from the day to maintain perspective.

I don't know what this looks like for you, but think about what re-energizes you and give yourself time at the beginning or end of each school day for inspiration. Take time to connect with others, tell stories, and laugh. Whatever it means for you, schedule time into your day for inspiration. When you do, you will find yourself better able to handle the stress and pace required for serving others.

Let's Wrap This Up

Where are you on the 20,000-day scale? What goals are you setting for yourself today and for the coming year? Yours may look completely different from mine. Maybe you are committed to reaching a new milestone in your physical health. Or maybe you have new goals for growing in relationships with your family. Today is only one day in this life you've been given, but it is an important day. Although you may not accomplish all the goals you set for yourself, you can accomplish many of them.

Now It's Your Turn

What practical actions can you take to make your days more productive? Commit to not wasting time on time-sucking activities. Set realistic boundaries. Schedule time for what matters. Use smart tools for scheduling. Prioritize and chunk your time. And allow time for inspiration. When you do, you give yourself a head start on making each day count.

CHAPTER 5

Your Friendships

How Are You Learning to Climb Together?

The Mountain-Climb: *I'm sure some people enjoy climbing alone, but I have found that the hardest tasks are more easily accomplished when you combine your strength with the strengths of others. The combination can be both inspiring and empowering. And isolation is often an enemy to progress.*

When I was in college, I had my first experience with mountain climbing. I was traveling in Guatemala for a summer missions outreach. One morning, my team members and I woke up before dawn and rode a bus to the base of an active volcano. We were a team of about twenty college students, and we decided to begin our climb in the dark so that we could summit the mountain at sunrise.

The night before, our team leader had talked to us about the climb. He explained how difficult the terrain would be as well as the altitude changes. He encouraged us to find team members whom we could stay with on the hike. He cautioned us that climbing was just as much emotional as it was physical and that we must be committed to finishing as the last 100 meters of the climb would be the hardest.

This past week, I was talking to my wife about friendships. She had just been reading the book, *Friendships Don't Just Happen! The Guide to Creating a Meaningful Circle of Girl Friends* by Shantel Nelson. In the book, Nelson refers to a study released on friendship in 2008 by professors from four universities called the "Social Support and the Perception of Geographical Slant" in the *Journal of Experimental Social Psychology*. Participants in the study were asked to estimate the incline of a hill in front of them. Over and over again, those who were accompanied by a friend (or even thought of a friend) estimated the hill to be less steep than participants who were alone. The researchers concluded that: "This research demonstrates that an interpersonal phenomenon, social support, can influence visual perception," (Schnall, Simone, et al., 2008, para. 1).

It may seem like common sense that the support or presence of a friend encourages or positively motivates you. But this study suggests that the presence of a friend actually changes your physical and emotional perceptions.

Why Your Friendships Matter

One of the biggest challenges I find with educators is their tendency to work in isolation. While you may be surrounded by students all day, it doesn't mean you have the interpersonal support or presence of other adults to help you navigate difficult moments. This is one reason why I believe so many educators struggle with burnout. The need for relationships is one reason high-performing schools foster an environment of professional learning—teams of educators who meet regularly and work interdependently to find shared solutions for student learning.

Contrary to popular opinion, I do not believe you can be or do your best simply through self-reliance. Yes, grit is necessary to succeed, but I believe educators struggle with enormous pressure to be "superhero" educators. During my first year as an assistant principal, for instance, I carried around a yellow note pad as I walked my school. When teachers or students stopped to talk, I would jot down any concerns or questions they had. Then I would spend time after school following up on any of these issues that needed to be addressed. In my mind, I was being the kind of principal I had always dreamed of having as a teacher: the person whom could be available any time to find solutions, answer questions, or put out situational fires.

> The need for relationships is one reason high-performing schools foster an environment of professional learning—teams of educators who meet regularly and work interdependently to find shared solutions for student learning.

What I didn't realize was the misperception I had about my role. I thought leadership meant being a kind of "super-person" who could single handedly manage the most difficult situations of a school so that teachers could teach, and students could learn. Although I was personally responsible for the outcomes related to the biggest challenges in my schools, I was missing out on an important truth: the biggest challenges in our schools are best solved together, not alone. As I thought back to my time in the classroom, I realized that some of my best learning moments came from finding solutions together with my students, relying on other teachers for feedback, and admitting when I needed help.

Over the years as a new administrator, I realized that when I finally reached out to my colleagues, friends, and even students for feedback and support, I discovered better solutions.

Let me give you another example. One year I confided in another educator my tendency to work late hours and miss mealtimes with my family. So, this colleague began to hold me accountable. As she left each day with plenty of time to be home with her family, she would stop by and say, "Okay, Will. Whatever you're working on can wait. Your family needs you more than this school does. Go home." That small act of accountability pushed me out the door and helped me increase my time with my wife and kids.

Why are friendships essential to your own journey ahead? Here are four reasons you should rely on the power of your friendships and trust others both in your personal life and as a school leader:

1. Friendships provide accountability.

One of the biggest dangers of any work is the tendency to forget you don't know it all. Just because you have advanced degrees or a position of authority does not automatically qualify you as an expert in everything. At the risk of again sounding like your grandfather, let me just say it like it is: Stay humble. And one of the best ways to do that is by surrounding yourself with others who have permission to give you honest feedback.

In a school setting and in your personal life, you need others with whom you regularly connect for updates, sharing, or simply checking in. And this happens best when you schedule time for it. As a teacher, I built time into my lunch schedule each day to meet with trusted colleagues for feedback, laughter, and reflection. As a high school principal, my secretary and I had a standing meeting every Tuesday at 9 a.m. We would compare calendars, discuss next the steps on projects or schedules, and I could listen to any concerns she was aware of that needed my attention.

I also scheduled meetings with my administrative team members, department chairs, professional learning teams, student leadership groups, and district leadership because I valued their feedback.

> You may work faster alone, but you always accomplish more meaningful outcomes when you include others on your journey.

Some of these conversations can be short and informal. When pressed for time or serious collaboration, set a time limit on these meetings, take notes on what you discuss, and follow-up afterwards with any decisions that were made. But create a framework of accountability so that you have consistent conversations, feedback, and accountability for the work ahead.

In my personal life, I have a group of men with whom I meet once a month. Together we discuss issues affecting our lives and families. These men have become a source of encouragement and help during times of family or personal crises. Think about how you can rely on those around you for accountability. You may work faster alone, but you always accomplish more meaningful outcomes when you include others on your journey.

2. Friendships provide life support.

When I was a new teacher, one of the veteran teachers in my school had an older sister who passed away. We gathered some money as a faculty and gave him a gift to help cover the travel expenses he would have to attend her funeral out of state. I was in my mid-twenties and had never lost a sibling. But I remember standing with him in the teacher's lunch room as his closest colleagues hugged him while he cried.

In 2010, my older brother died of a heart-attack at age forty-five. I was thirty-nine at the time, and I remember the comfort and strength I found in just having others near me who cared. Whether at school or at home, we need community. Some of the most difficult moments you will face in education will be managing crises in the lives of students, co-workers, or members of your school community. And friendships will often be the glue that holds your community together during those most difficult times.

3. Friendships provide reflection.

In the day-to-day work of serving others, you always have room for growth and improvement. And one way to keep growing is by reflecting with trusted friends. In Dan Pink's bestselling book *When: The Scientific Secrets of Perfect Timing,* he talks about how common it is for people to make wrong decisions at certain times of the day—especially when they are tired or emotionally drained (Pink, 2019).

Have you ever considered how important it is to contemplate your decision-making tendencies? Because everyone is prone to making wrong calls in emotionally draining situations, it is important to reflect with others when you are making important decisions that affect others. For instance, whenever you're facing a scenario you may have never faced before, you should consider reaching out to a trusted colleague. It is better to reflect with others rather than make hasty decisions and regret them later.

Reflection is also a powerful way to make better decisions. At the end of each school year, we had a practice of pulling together our office and administrative staff for debrief meetings. This allowed us to talk through any actions that needed to be taken in the days ahead as we wrapped up the school year as well as reflected on tasks just completed. We would keep a running Google Doc of our last ten days of school together and share the tasks that needed to be completed together. By simply reflecting together, discussing what was working and what was not, we could set new goals and improve the way we worked.

Reflection also happens daily. As you finish a lesson or a team meeting, reflect with others on what worked and what didn't. One of the benefits of connecting with others through Professional Learning

Communities, whether in person or online, is the ability to share ideas, reference good books, and discuss educational practices.

One of the reasons I enjoy blogging and podcasting is the ability to reflect each week on what I'm learning. Reflecting with others helps you see things you wouldn't normally see on your own. Your friendships allow you to reflect with others for personal growth.

4. Friendships bring out the best in others.

This may seem obvious but still needs to be said: You are not the best version of yourself alone. Yes, solitude and self-reflection are important parts of personal growth. But so is community. And in a culture that prizes independence and self-reliance, we often forget how important it is to have others around us.

There is a story that I love about friendship, involving C.S. Lewis, the author of *The Chronicles of Narnia*. Lewis was friends with J.R.R. Tolkien, the author of *The Hobbit* and *The Lord of the Rings* trilogy, and the two of them had a mutual friend named Charles Williams. When Charles died, Lewis wrote the following:

> In each of my friends there is something that only some other friend can fully bring out. By myself I am not large enough to call the whole man into activity; I want other lights than my own to show all his facets. Now that Charles is dead, I shall never again see Ronald's [Tolkien's] reaction to a specifically Charles joke. Far from having more of Ronald, having him "to myself" now that Charles is away, I have less of Ronald...In this, Friendship exhibits a glorious "nearness by resemblance" to heaven itself... (Keller, 2016, p. 141).

You have others in your life who can see parts of you that you are unable to see yourself. And you have attributes that may be best displayed with one person over another. Keep this in mind as you remember the importance of connecting with friends, family, and community members. Sometimes we need one another to see the best in one another.

Let's Wrap This Up

When I was climbing my first mountain, I remember reaching the last 100 meters and realizing the climb would be difficult. Because we were climbing a volcano, the final ascent was nothing but black rock and pebbles. With each step, I climbed two or three feet and slid back a foot or more. So, to ascend 100 meters, I was really climbing 300 meters as I lunged forward, clutching onto the sliding rocks around me as I slid back and then lunged forward again.

I had partnered with one of the girls on the team for the final climb. About halfway up, she said she couldn't continue. "Yes, you can!" I said. "We'll do this together." All around us were other team members who had paired up. We were clutching hands or placing our palms into the heels of boots in front us to create footholds for one another. It was a hard climb that I'm not sure I could have made if I had been alone. Together, we finished the climb, stood atop the peak, and enjoyed an amazing sunrise.

I don't know what kind of climb you are facing. But it is safe to say that you are more likely to finish it with strength because of the encouragement of friends. Just as researchers have discovered that even our perceptions and attitudes change in the presence of friends (or even thinking of them), our ability to face the hills ahead will be much greater when we welcome the accountability, life-support, reflection, and discovery that happens through relationships.

Now It's Your Turn

Who are people in your life whom you can rely on for accountability? How can you schedule time to reflect with others? Who are some friends you know that bring out the better parts of you? Reach out to them today and tell them you're thinking about them. And in the school year ahead, commit to serving your community together.

CHAPTER 6

Your Spirituality

How Is Faith Influencing You?

Newborn baby: *No parent can look at a newborn baby without a profound sense of wonder and awe. And nothing can prepare you for the overwhelming emotions you feel for your children. How often do you consider the power of your Heavenly Father's care for your faith and spiritual growth?*

This past summer, I was on an airplane with my oldest daughter, Emily, who had just finished her first year of college and was enjoying her summer break. Being with her brought back a lot of memories. At the time, she was staring out the window at the landscape of clouds below while we flew to a conference together in Chicago. As I watched her, I recalled the moment of her birth and moments from her growing up over the years. I thought about how hard is to explain the kind of love you have for your children.

I'm a father of four, and with each one, I have had such deep emotions that words fail to describe the feelings. When I held Emily in my arms for the first time, I remember the overwhelming affection I felt—and the thought that I had no idea what I was doing. But I also discovered I had no idea how deep a father's love could be. Thinking about a father's love helps me reflect on my spiritual growth.

Your beliefs guide your thinking and life decisions. The bedrock for my beliefs comes from my background and experience as a Christian—the belief in a Heavenly Father who cares deeply for His children, has revealed Himself through the holy Scriptures, and is reconciling all creation to Himself through the life, death, and resurrection of Jesus. I realize my personal experience and beliefs about God may differ from yours, but I'd still like you to consider some reasons why spirituality matters in personal development, whether you are also a Christian or a follower of any other religion or faith practice. Even if you are non-religious, you may find these ideas helpful in understanding your students or colleagues whose faith plays a strong role in their lives.

4 Reasons Your Faith Matters

1. Faith provides a bedrock of assurance.

We live in a world of uncertainty, and our experiences increase anxiety and stress because of these uncertain environments (both globally and locally). Our children, for instance, live with risks and dangers (global terrorism, school shootings, and pandemics, to name a few) that many previous generations did not face. These issues are amplified by immediate news and social media coverage. It should come as no surprise when our students (and adults for that matter) are so stressed out. At the same time, human experience has always included risk. In every aspect of your life, you have to accept that there are some situations and experiences that are beyond your control.

52

But when faced with any difficult scenario—like counseling an abused child or struggling through the death of a loved one—no amount of self-talk replaces the kind of assurance that faith provides for me. Spirituality has been identified as a necessary resource for building resilience (Goldhill, 2016). Walking by faith does not mean pretending. Instead, it means placing your trust in something or someone who promises hope—a belief that your circumstances are ultimately under God's control.

This does not mean that I expect my students or education colleagues to share my faith. Instead, I can step into each day (whether the day is one of inspiration or crisis) knowing that I can move forward with courage and assurance.

2. Faith provides a measure of perspective.

I think it is important to ask yourself the question: Who are you ultimately trusting for the outcomes you hope to see in your work or life? Your ability to self-reflect and rely on others will provide you with growth and improved outcomes, but many of your outcomes have nothing to do with you.

My grandfather was a farmer. I would ride the tractor with him as he planted corn or soybeans. I noticed how hard he worked to till the soil, select good grain, apply fertilizer, and plant in early spring and summer. But there were a number of elements he could not control. First, he planted outdoors, not in a greenhouse, and he was unable to control the weather. Second, the rain was not within his control. But most importantly, he had no power over the seeds. Yes, those seeds were helped by being surrounded with the right conditions, but sprouting and growth was never guaranteed.

In the classroom or schoolhouse, you can place your students in the best conditions possible for personal or academic growth. But you also have to trust in the elements beyond your control. Frankly, some of you reading this have encountered others in your work or life who seemed beyond help at times. As I've met with students who appeared to be in conditions beyond my reach, I've had to learn to trust in what I cannot see. Not every situation turns out exactly as you plan, but when you trust God for the ultimate outcome, you are practicing the same wisdom as a good farmer.

3. Faith provides a community of strong support.

Over the years, I have managed a number of crises involving student illnesses or deaths. Some of them were unexpected circumstances, like car accidents or murder, while others were the result of disease. When you face moments of crisis, your students and teachers need to know they belong to a school where empathy and compassion are available. And communities of faith add an additional layer of support.

> When you face moments of crisis, your students and teachers need to know they belong to a school where empathy and compassion are available.

Most schools provide students with access to counselors or therapists. For your students of faith, a clergy member may also know them through interactions in places of worship. Over the years, I have seen ministers, for instance, who provide places for school communities to hold candle-light ceremonies during a time of crisis—places to gather for community prayers. These experiences may not be ones in which all students or families participate, but they provide powerful moments of support, encouragement, and healing for grieving loved ones.

In addition, faith-filled communities can be powerful partners. Some of the best volunteers and supporters of schools come from faith-based community members eager to see their local schools thriving and flourishing. And in my own experience, I do not know how I would have survived the normal walks of life without the people I gather with regularly for worship and community.

4. Faith provides healthy context for your leadership.
Recently, I heard some insightful research from Professor Scott Barry Kaufman from the University of Pennsylvania. He spoke on the topic of "*Cultivating Grit from Within*". In his speech, Kaufman explained research from Maslow's hierarchy of needs, with some interesting new definitions Kaufman in an upcoming book.

Kaufman explained that one of the areas Maslow explored in his hierarchy was self-actualization (Maslow, 1954). The traditional Maslow model is represented in the following diagram:

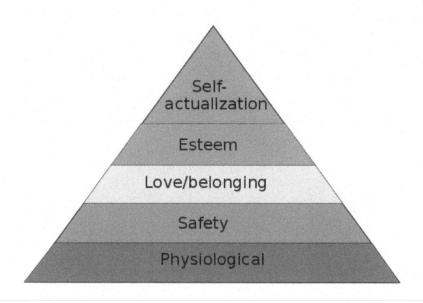

But in his later writings, Maslow talked more about transcendence, the highest level of human experience where people pursue something equivalent to reaching for the infinite (Kaufman, 2017). In later Maslow models, he added transcendence above self-actualization. Kaufman reminded his listeners that ultimate learning experiences involve discovery, awe, and wonder—not just receiving information, but finding inspiration.

> ultimate learning experiences involve discovery, awe, and wonder—not just receiving information, but finding inspiration.

The application for me is simple: As an educator, how can I expect teachers and students to tap into moments of inspiration and awe if I don't value those experiences myself? Let me ask another important question: Why do you step into your school each morning? I do not believe it is because you want to simply earn a salary or because you love being in control of students. If so, you will seldom find long-term satisfaction or meaning in your work. I believe you step into your school each day because you want to be a part of creating the kind of community where others can be inspired to grow, learn, discover, and flourish. Faith provides a healthy context for this perspective.

Let's Wrap This Up

My daughter Emily was born six and a half weeks premature, a healthy five pounds, eleven ounces. She was hospitalized in a neonatal intensive care unit while her lungs developed and we waited to bring her home.

Neonatal care specialists will tell you there is no safer place than a mother's womb during pregnancy. But when a baby comes early, it is comforting to see the specialized care premature babies receive. During her first days, Emily was placed in a small crib and connected to wires that measured her heart rate and blood pressure, and she was fed oxygen through small tubes that were inserted into her tiny nose. As the days continued, her lungs strengthened, and she was disconnected from the oxygen so that we could hold and help feed her.

As wonderful and miraculous as neonatal care is for premature babies, there was something those cribs, machines, and monitors could not provide. Nothing could replace the love that my wife and I gave her. Whether it was stroking her little back with my forefinger while she slept, or watching my wife hold and feed her for the first time, we were radiating a kind of affection that I believe worked as deeply on her as the medical treatments she received. What a joy it was to bring her home two and half weeks later. And what a joy it has been to watch her grow from a healthy baby into an amazing young woman.

So often, I hear educators talk about their work as a calling. I think it is more apt to say your life is a calling. Whenever you confront the realities of life—your relationships, work, or health—you will inevitably hit walls of discouragement, isolation, and struggle. But when you think about how an eternal Father offers an affection that touches you at the deepest core of your being, you can know you are never alone. You can have assurance about those things beyond your control, perspective for the journey ahead, support from others in a community of faith, and meaning that goes far beyond the moment you are presently experiencing.

Now It's Your Turn

As you pause to reflect on the kind of motivation you need as an educator, take some additional time to reflect on the eternal significance of your work. How can you make time to accept what is beyond your control by relying in faith for the ultimate good to happen? How can you support others in their struggles or difficulties by pointing them to an assurance that is both present and eternal?

CHAPTER 7

Your Resources

How Are You Utilizing What You Steward?

Parachutes: *Parachutes are not something most of us will use in life. I've never had to jump from a plane. But I'd be glad to have a parachute alongside me if one were ever needed. At the same time, I remember playing with parachutes in elementary school. My teacher used one as a game for tossing balls in the air. The same fabric that was woven together to save lives also provided a lot of joy for a room full of children.*

The other day, I was talking to a friend who ran track in high school. When he was at his fastest, he could run a mile in four minutes and thirty seconds. Even though he was naturally fast, he learned to increase his speed through practice. He said his coach made him wear a parachute during practice to build strength and speed.

I was thinking about what it would feel like to run with a parachute. The weight and pull against your shoulders and legs would be almost unbearable. But imagine how fast you would run once the resistance was removed! Sometimes I view managing resources like wearing a parachute. If you are running with a lot of financial stress like personal debt, for instance, you may feel the pull and weight of trying to move ahead with life. If you've found a level of financial stability, however, you may see money as a parachute that is helping you land safely when needed. For most people, money seems to act both ways.

When my wife and I first finished college, we began married life with a lot of college debt. Now that I'm older, I realize that we were not alone. Just recently, the Federal Reserve announced that outstanding student debt for U.S. residents has now topped $1.5 trillion (Berman, 2018). Thankfully, early in our marriage, we discovered some great resources on personal finance from authors like Ron Blue and Dave Ramsey. With a lot of discipline and planning, we were able to pay down debt, save for emergencies, and make a down payment for our first home.

Throughout the years, however, we've still had demands on our money that have required us to refocus or relearn some of those same lessons. Money seems to be an area of life most people keep very private. You may find it uncomfortable to reflect on your own personal spending, saving, and budgeting habits in a book for educators. However, your willingness (or resistance) to talk about money may influence the way you think and live.

How does your personal money management influence your life as an educator? I know it may seem odd to include a chapter on money to those who have chosen a career of service. But how you manage your resources plays an important part in the decisions you will be making as an educator and for future positions you may consider. Obviously, when you are responsible for managing your classroom or school resources like activity accounts or school budgets, you must practice strong accountability and responsibility. But in this chapter, I want to focus on how your personal finances—and your mindset about managing your resources—also influences your professional effectiveness. Entire books have been written on this subject, so let me just offer four ways I believe your attitudes about and practices regarding personal finances matters as an educator:

1. Your money management allows you freedom (or lack of freedom) in your career choices.

Early in my education career, I was talking to a friend about how I was struggling with the leadership and support at my school and was unsure what to do next. I no longer felt like I thrived in that school environment. My friend patiently listened to my struggles and then said, "Will, we don't live in a communist country. If there's a better opportunity for you out there, go for it."

That simple statement was a wake-up call for me, reminding me that I had a choice. But during that discussion, I also realized I had the freedom to look at options because of how my wife and I were managing our finances. By living within our means and saving for future expenses, I also had the freedom and perspective to look at other job options without as much fear for the future.

Some people worry about their employers knowing they are considering other occupations for fear they may lose their jobs. Thankfully, I've not worked in environments like that. But even if I had, I still believe that healthy practices related to money management allow for a more peaceful perspective when making important career choices.

For example, the other day I was listening to the story of a man who lived in an economically depressed area of his city. He gave up a job making nine dollars an hour to work for a better company making fourteen dollars an hour. The catch, however, was his new commute to work. His better paying job was fifteen miles across town. Because he was limited to using public transportation, his commute required several hours of travel to and from work each day. In essence, he was devoting several hours each day to travel and sleeping only four hours a night to make an additional thirty-two dollars a day.

I know his situation is also a complicated example of systematic economic conditions many people face beyond their own control. But the point is this: sometimes it is possible to be unnecessarily burdened by your financial decisions when you are so overwhelmed by circumstances that keep you from seeing other options. For instance, if the same man could have found part-time work at nine dollars an hour for four more hours a day, he could have made an additional $36 a day, stayed closer to home, and gotten more sleep.

Obviously, I did not choose the career of an educator to become wealthy. When I stepped into the field of education, I realized my teaching income would be limited by salary schedules or district policies beyond my control. One area I could control, however, was the management of the resources I had at my disposal. By viewing your finances as leverage, instead of just as disposable income, you will often have more wisdom, flexibility and choice when considering the options before you.

2. Your money management helps you set goals for your time and energy.

Seven years ago, I was looking at my growing family and anticipating my oldest daughter leaving for college. Looking ahead, I was aware that I needed to increase my income potential. Unlike many of my peers, I was not interested in becoming a school superintendent (no offense to all my friends who are).

When I looked at the financial landscape, I had a choice. I could despair, or I could invest my time toward expanding opportunities. I love to write and wanted to share stories and lessons with other educators. So, I began dedicating time, usually in the evenings or very early mornings, to writing at least 500 words per week to share as a blog post. Seven years later, I have three books in print and a weekly podcast. I have spoken, presented or provided keynote addresses at more than fifty events in more than a dozen states across the U.S. My time commitment influenced my career opportunities.

When I began that process, the economy was in a recession, unemployment was at an all-time high, and the prospects of seeing a raise in my salary was unsure for the short-term. But I chose to ignore all of those obstacles by realizing I still had control over my time and energy.

I realize you may face bigger challenges than others because of your unique economic, political, or social dynamics. Educators often face enormous stress because of the income limits involved in our profession. As a young educator, I spent years teaching summer school, painting houses, mowing yards, or teaching weekend adult-education courses for extra income. But each step along the way, I tried to have a plan for managing the resources at my disposal. When you approach your resources with a mindset of what is possible, not just what is not possible, you have a clearer perspective on your time investments.

3. Your money management reminds you that resources are temporary and managing them is a gift.
No one is really self-sufficient. Most individuals with financial independence have exchanged their time and effort for the rewards they enjoy. That's how money works. You create something of value, and others are willing to exchange something valuable for it. As your work creates value for others, you earn an income. But even the most successful person will eventually lose the ability to produce. Ultimately, your money and possessions are only temporary. As one of my old country music favorites, Ricky Skaggs, would say, "You can't take it with you when you go."

Years ago, I heard a story about a preacher who was asked to lunch by a wealthy landowner. During their meal, the landowner expressed his disagreement with a sermon he had heard from the preacher about God owning everything. The preacher politely listened but did not argue back. After lunch, the man took the preacher on a long drive across acres of pastures and fields. At the top of a hill overlooking his property, the man said, "I've worked my whole life to acquire this land. Now how can you tell me I don't really own all this?" The preacher was silent for a while, and then he finally replied, "Can you ask me that question again in a hundred years?"

Whatever resources you currently have, you are really only the manager of possessions someone else will own when you are gone. We

> But when you realize what you have is only temporary, you are able to appreciate it more and realize its value is in how it is used, not how much it is worth.

all face the danger of turning our possessions into symbols of self-identity or self-worth. But when you realize what you have is only temporary, you are able to appreciate it more and realize its value is in how it is used, not how much it is worth.

That same mindset helps whether you are talking about income, relationships, talents, or knowledge. If you keep those resources to yourself, you are missing out on the greatest value of having them. And that leads to the last point...

4. Your money management gives you context for your work and your calling.
It is important to remember the reason why we work and manage resources. Ultimately, our resources are put to best use when they are helping others. But generosity is not just measured by how you give your money, although it is a good indicator of your priorities. You have lots of ways you can express generosity.

A few years ago, my family faced a number of emergencies that became bigger burdens than we could manage on our own. During that time, my son Jack was diagnosed with a rare disease that hospitalized him for two weeks. His recovery overlapped with Halloween, so we simply planned to miss out on the festivities that year.

Unbeknownst to us, a friend of ours posted a message on Facebook Halloween morning that said, "There's a boy at St. Francis Hospital, room 329, who needs to celebrate Halloween today. Don't let him be disappointed." Soon friends, as well as people we had never met, began to stop by Jack's room with gifts, candy, video games, and other treats. Jack was so excited to see each person. By the end of the day, every table, counter, and windowsill in the room was covered with bags of goodies. My family still talks about that Halloween day. We were facing a difficult situation that was beyond our control, but the generosity of friends and strangers surrounded us with emotional support.

We were also facing the financial burdens from hospital expenses not covered by insurance. Through conversations, the hospital staff encouraged us to submit a letter requesting help. A few weeks later, the hospital sent back a letter explaining they had forgiven the remaining bills for Jack's stay.

It is humbling when you face times when your own resources or abilities cannot provide everything you need. Most people are fiercely independent. But when you are the recipient of generosity, it is not only humbling but also a good reminder of the support you can bring others when they have needs. In the end, the greatest benefit of wisely managing your resources is the ability to help others.

Let's Wrap This Up

There is another story about parachutes that I love to tell. One day at my school office, I found a handwritten card in my mailbox from a senior student thanking me for "packing her parachute." I was curious about what she meant, and then I saw inside the envelope. She had placed a cut-out piece of parachute cloth and a folded-up copy of an excerpt by a man named Charlie Plumb, which read:

Recently, I was sitting in a restaurant in Kansas City. A man about two tables away kept looking at me. I didn't recognize him. A few minutes into our meal he stood up and walked over to my table, looked down at me, pointed his finger in my face and said, "You're Captain Plumb."

I looked up and I said, "Yes sir, I'm Captain Plumb."

He said, "You flew jet fighters in Vietnam. You were on the air-craft carrier Kitty Hawk. You were shot down. You parachuted into enemy hands and spent six years as a prisoner of war."

I said, "How in the world did you know all that?"

He replied, "Because, I packed your parachute."

I was speechless. I staggered to my feet and held out a very grate-ful hand of thanks. This guy came up with just the proper words. He grabbed my hand, he pumped my arm and said, "I guess it worked."

"Yes sir, indeed it did", I said, "and I must tell you I've said a lot of prayers of thanks for your nimble fingers, but I never thought I'd have the opportunity to express my gratitude in person."

He said, "Were all the panels there?"

"Well sir, I must shoot straight with you," I said. "Of the eighteen panels that were supposed to be in that parachute, I had fifteen good ones. Three were torn, but it wasn't your fault, it was mine. I jumped

out of that jet fighter at a high rate of speed, close to the ground. That's what tore the panels in the chute. It wasn't the way you packed it. Let me ask you a question: do you keep track of all the parachutes you pack?"

"No," he responded, "it's enough gratification for me just to know that I've served."

I didn't get much sleep that night. I kept thinking about that man. I kept wondering what he might have looked like in a Navy uniform—a Dixie cup hat, a bib in the back and bell bottom trousers. I wondered how many times I might have passed him on board the Kitty Hawk. I wondered how many times I might have seen him and not even said, "Good morning," "How are you?" or anything because, you see, I was a fighter pilot and he was just a sailor. How many hours did he spend on that long wooden table in the bowels of that ship weaving the shrouds and folding the silks of those chutes? I could have cared less...until one day my parachute came along and he packed it for me. So, the philosophical question here is this: How's your parachute packing coming along? Who looks to you for strength in times of need? And perhaps, more importantly, who are the special people in your life who provide you the encouragement you need when the chips are down? Perhaps it's time right now to give those people a call and thank them for packing your chute (Packing Your Parachute, 2013, para. 10).

In case you haven't been reminded lately, thank you for packing parachutes. And as you look at the way you manage your time and money, please do not feel guilty if you are struggling at the moment. Remember your resources are simply commodities you've been given. Your time, attention, affection and compassion are still more important than your bank account. And the way you give these tangible and intangible commodities to help others will not go unnoticed. But managing your resources well does matter.

When you do, you may have more freedom in your choices, more intentionality with your time, more perspective on your work, and more opportunities for generosity toward others. As a result, you will keep packing parachutes for others and will have the ability to recognize when others are packing yours.

Now It's Your Turn

What is one way you can rethink how money management influences your time and energy? What is one small way you can use your resources to brighten someone's day or lighten his or her load? When was the last time you paused to thank someone for the ways they helped you with their time, attention, or resources?

CHAPTER 8

Your Intimacy

How Are Your Most Important Relationships Guiding You?

Rowing: *If you've ever rowed a boat, you know that paddling against the water on the right side will steer your boat to the left. When two people are rowing, they will often row together so that their synchronized movements keep them headed in the right direction. Rowing together is much easier than rowing against one another. And together, you always have the potential of going faster and farther.*

In 2018, my wife and I enjoyed time away from home, celebrating our twenty-fifth wedding anniversary in Lake Tahoe, Nevada. One afternoon, we drove to Emerald Bay, a cove nestled a mile below the mountain highway. We hiked the trail and rented a kayak. When we pushed away from shore, I was immediately struck by the clarity of the water. Gray mountains covered in tall pines and shrubs formed a semi-circle around the cove. As we looked across the water, the blue skies shown across the clear, spring-fed surface with a silvery-blue hue. My wife, Missy, was sitting up front, her bare legs and feet extended across the front of the boat as she soaked in the sunlight. We rowed ahead until we approached the round boulders of a small island where we stopped for photos and selfies. This was a happy moment, and we were doing what we loved most—being outdoors together.

When I was a junior in college, I had a Christmas party to attend at the end of my fall semester, and bringing a date was a requirement for attending the party. At the time, I wasn't dating anyone, but I asked myself what I realize now was one of the most important questions in my life: Who would be the "perfect girl" to ask on this date? I started making a mental list. It should be a girl who was pretty and smart. I wanted her to care about her spiritual life and be dedicated to a strong personal vision. It was a tall order. On top of it all, I could only offer a fun, non-romantic evening with no expectations of a second date.

My first memory of Missy had been after my freshman year in college. We had attended some summer trainings together, but I didn't really know her. Over the next couple of years, I would see her at various gatherings. She was fun-loving, and other girls looked to her as a leader.

During my junior year, Missy's younger brother lived on my floor. I remember a photo he kept of her on his desk. One day, I stopped to look at it. *Wow*, I thought. *She's pretty*. I started paying more attention.

Six weeks before the Christmas party, Missy and I were working together at a campus event. I didn't want to miss the opportunity to be the first guy to ask her. So, after working up the courage, I decided to go for it. What could I lose?

"Hey," I said as I walked up to the table where she sat. She looked up and smiled. "I have a question I want to ask about your...calendar," I started.

"Okay?" she glanced at me curiously and pulled out a planner from her bag.

I thought hard about what say next. "I was wondering what you might be doing on December 6th? I mean, I know that's a long time from now, but I wanted to see if you had anything scheduled then?"

"Well," she paused then thumbed through the pages and stopped. "Actually, I don't have anything planned on that day."

"Cool," I said, "Could I...pencil something in for you?"

She smiled and handed it to me. I took a pencil from the table and wrote: *Men's RA Christmas Party, 6 p.m. – Will Parker.*

And then I handed it back. She looked at the page for a moment and then back at me.

"Could you go?" I asked.

It was the longest moment of my life, and suddenly, I realized how much I wanted her to say yes.

"OK," she said. "I don't have anything else going on then. So, I'd be glad to go."

Fast forward twenty years later. Missy and I were standing on the banks of the Illinois River in Eastern Oklahoma. Our four kids were skipping rocks on the water, and we were watching as the sun set orange above towering trees on the opposite bank. I sat down at a nearby picnic table, and everyone gathered around.

"I have an announcement to make," I said. "You know I've been offered a new job as an executive director for my principal association, and I've decided to take it."

Emily, my oldest daughter, began to cry. Missy and I looked at each other, and then we all gathered around her for a group hug. Emily had just graduated from Skiatook, the school I had worked at for the past ten years, and we had a lot of memories there. It would be hard to say goodbye.

We talked for a long time as a family about how the next year might look. Each family member took a turn talking about the ups and downs for the coming school year. Soon, we had settled what the path forward would look like. As our children walked ahead of us, we watched them strolling across the grass and through the trees back toward our cabin.

Why Your Most Important Relationships Matter

Not every moment in our marriage and family life has been filled with blissful memories like these. Marriage is a series of ups and downs. For every happy moment you share, you also experience sleepless nights, unresolved conflicts, broken promises, and strained commitments. But for us, the investment has been worth it.

I've shared before about the first few years of our marriage, when I transitioned from teaching to school administration. The over-commitment to school hurt my marriage and my health. Thankfully, my wife had the courage to tell me that I had become a shell of the man I used to be. This wake-up call forced me to rethink my priorities in every area of my life. And my marriage was one of them.

In the book *The 5 Love Languages: The Secret to Love that Lasts*, author Gary Chapman talks about the importance of understanding the specific ways others receives love. Maybe it's quality time or giving something that expresses appreciation. Perhaps it's physical affection or acts of service. Sometimes it's verbal praise. Chapman explains how each time you communicate love to someone else in his or her own language, you make deposits into his or her love bank. Each time you fail to invest, you are making withdrawals. The equation is simple, when you make more meaningful deposits than withdrawals into your most important relationships, you increase the potential to grow closer over time (Chapman, 2017).

Healthy Relationships Means a Healthier You

You may be reading this as a single person. Please know this chapter is not my attempt to convince anyone that marriage is better than being single. Committed friendships or other family relationships provide deep, supportive outcomes for singles just as healthy marriages may for others. Whatever those most important relationships look like for you, they matter—whether they include commitments among parents to children, grandparents to grandchildren, aunts/uncles to nephews/nieces, or close friends to other close friends.

At the same time, I do want to speak from my own experience, which includes my marriage and family, and how those takeaways may apply to your most intimate relationships. Long-term, committed relationships have healthy benefits. For instance, Dr. Robert H. Shmerling, the faculty editor for Harvard Health Publishing, talked about the benefits of marriage in a post on November 30, 2016 in his blog at Health. Harvard.edu. I think his words may also apply to other deeply supportive relationships.

He writes:

...there is fascinating — and compelling — research suggesting that married people enjoy better health than single people. For example, as compared with those who are single, those who are married tend to

- live longer
- have fewer strokes and heart attacks
- have a lower chance of becoming depressed
- be less likely to have advanced cancer at the time of diagnosis and more likely to survive cancer for a longer period of time
- survive a major operation more often.

This doesn't mean that just being married automatically provides these health benefits. People in stressful, unhappy marriages may be worse off than a single person who is surrounded by supportive and caring friends, family, and loved ones. Interestingly, many of these health benefits are more pronounced for married men than for married women (Shmerling, 2016).

An important application of Shmerling's point is this: Healthy, supportive relationships are important and worth the investment. They are often the context for meaningful life outcomes that will carry you far beyond your job title or occupation. Let's face it. As educators, we often pour our lives into serving others. The nature of our work is to prepare students or other educators with the capacity, knowledge, and skills to live without us. Educators work in an environment of building relationships, but the vast majority of our students will move on once another class advances or graduates. Our colleagues often move into other positions, transfer to other schools, or relocate to other cities. Those relationships matter, but what relationships in your life do you see as permanent and long-term? And how do you encourage a mindset of prioritizing those persons whom you will still want with you long after your time in education is over?

6 Questions for Reflecting on Your Most Important Relationships

Although these questions are important for any meaningful relationship, I would like to speak directly from my own experience and from the context of twenty-seven years of marriage. If you are not married, perhaps you will think about how these lessons may apply to your own meaningful relationships or perhaps those of your married colleagues. If you are married, when was the last time you took inventory of your commitment to your relationship? Here are six questions to consider:

74

1. When was the last time you revisited your marriage vows?
Deep relationships are rooted in trust—whether that is a best friend who has committed to be there no matter what or a parent who shows up to every school play. That's why the traditions around marriage, for instance, include vows. For my married readers, if haven't read your marriage vows lately, pull them out or listen closely at the next wedding you attend. Most likely they'll say something like this:

"I, ___, take thee, ___, ..., to have and to hold, from this day forward, for better, for worse, for richer, for poorer, in sickness and in health, to love and to cherish, till death do us part, according to God's holy ordinance; and thereto I pledge thee my faith [or] pledge myself to you," (The Knot, 2019).

Obviously, some commitments do not last long-term for a variety of reasons beyond your control. But promises are important, and if you really mean what you say, your loved ones should know you prioritize them above everyone else in your life. As an educator, this can be a tall order when so many others are asking for your time and attention. But if promises matter, then it should be assumed that your most important relationships have a commitment greater than your work.

2. Are you giving your most important relationship first place over your work?
Giving most important relationships first place with your time and commitment has a lot of implications. First it means that the thoughts and opinions of those you love really matter. This doesn't mean you never debate or disagree with them. But it means their opinions always matter. Give your loved ones the respect they deserve when offering your suggestions, feedback, or advice. As you give priority to their feedback, you will save yourself a lot of pitfalls because they often see things you are blind to.

In every major career move I've made, for instance, my wife and family have weighed the pros and cons of accepting the new position together. Staying unified in major decisions doesn't mean agreeing on every point. But it does mean not moving ahead until you're in overall agreement. Yes, this also means compromise. And learning to compromise equals healthier relationships.

> Staying unified in major decisions doesn't mean agreeing on every point. But it does mean not moving ahead until you're in overall agreement.
>
>

3. Are you committed through the highs and lows?

No matter how much you love someone, you will go through seasons of ups and downs. Don't let how you feel at any given moment determine your long-term commitment to your promises. Promises and vows are kept regardless of how you feel. But here's a secret. When you act in response to the promises you've made, the right feelings almost always follow. This is especially important in romance and sex, for instance.

Our culture is obsessed with the idea of being led by your feelings. When you spend years with another person, your feelings can change, often depending on your current season of life. Raising children or starting a new job is hard work. Facing disease or health problems can create major stress. If your commitment to your loved one is based on a love that is solid no matter the ups or downs, you will always find the feelings returning as you journey together with that unwavering commitment.

4. Are you willing to keep learning and cooperating?

Healthy relationships are honest relationships while also showing a lot of grace. Again, I want to speak from my own experience: One of the best decisions Missy and I made early in our marriage was taking a couple's communication course. We read the book *A Couple's Guide to Communication* by John Gottman. It was written in the 70's, but the skills we learned are still relevant today (Gottman, 1979).

We learned how to practice open postures when talking, how to ask better questions, and how to repeat ourselves until we really understand one another. Practicing how to resolve conflicts and working through difficult conversations has been a bedrock for us. During our first year of marriage, we scheduled a date every Saturday morning for space to talk through any questions or conflicts that had surfaced during the previous week. And over the years, that early practice taught us a lot of skills we still use today. These same communication skills have proven essential in the other important relationships we have developed.

5. Can you admit when you need help?

When you hit walls that you cannot seem to conquer, ask for help—whether that's reaching out to a trusted counselor or friend or whether it means simply stopping and praying with your loved one. It is also wise to reach out to others when you can't seem to resolve issues. I have learned this lesson the hard way many times. But when I am willing to admit I cannot find solutions to major disagreements, I am always surprised at what happens to my attitude. Just the simple act of admitting you need help is sometimes the game changer for moving ahead with a solution you and your loved one can both have a part in discovering together.

6. Are you investing in time together and celebrating milestones?

Some couples or family units set a scheduled date night every week. Although we have not done that in ours, we have tried to make it a priority to reconnect in the ways that matter for the both of us. For my wife, that means prioritizing quality time to just sit and talk. As a family, we also love to travel together. A couple of years ago, a good friend of mine lost his wife to a rare disease after thirty-five years of marriage. The one piece of advice he gave me was to go on vacation together every year, even if it was something you may have to finance later. The memories you create will be ones you hold on to for the rest of your life.

Let's Wrap This Up

This past week, I sat by the bedside of my mother-in-law who has Alzheimer's. She'd had complications with her medications that hospitalized her for a few days while her doctor adjusted her dosages. As she recovered, Missy and I took turns staying with her. One night, I was alone with her, and we talked about when I first met Missy.

Because her memory is fading, she looked at me a few minutes later and said, "Where is Missy?"

"She's gone home to the put the kids to bed," I explained.

As she drifted off to sleep, I realized that someday my wife or I could be taking care of the other while they lie in a hospital bed. Or it may be one of my children, another family member or a close friend sitting with me in my final years.

Old age will someday fade your strength and memories. And when that time comes, you will not be worried about your lessons plans, master schedule or whether you read all your emails. But you will care about your most intimate relationships.

On our trip to Emerald Bay, Missy and I walked the edge of the shore after boating. We stood ankle deep in the cool waters and watched as other boats and kayaks moved across the surface. The sands under our feet swirled with golden flecks. Ducks rested on a floating log nearby.

As she took photos with her phone, I thought about our decades of marriage together: losing our first pregnancy in miscarriage, holding her hand during the births of our four children, lighting the candles of toddler birthday parties, helping kids study for tests late at night, traveling the long roads to band camps, experiencing the joy and tears at graduations, and holding each other's hands by the gravesides of lost family members.

Through it all, we've often returned to the promises we made one another—promises to put the other ahead of our personal interests—promises that seem so old-fashioned in a world where you're often told that nothing is as important as your personal happiness and fulfillment.

Even in the busyness of school, think about your most important relationships. Make it a priority to revisit your promises, give your loved ones the priority they deserve, stay committed through the highs and lows, keep learning together, admit when you need help, and celebrate the milestones along the way. As you do, you will find the lessons from these most meaningful relationships will keep you humble and inspired as you keep rowing ahead together in serving others.

Now It's Your Turn

Think about your most important relationships. How can you make the time to keep them a priority? How can you encourage your fellow teachers and teammates to prioritize time with their loved ones, spouses and families? Even in the busyness of school, what are some routines or practices you follow for staying connected to the ones you love?

CHAPTER 9

Your Future
How Are You Providing Others with Stronger Focus?

A Stronger Focus: *Sometimes we forget we have six senses. What you see, taste, touch, hear, smell, and feel are powerful reminders of why each moment counts, if you're willing to slow down and pay attention to these obvious but often missed experiences. Even if you have the gift of good eye sight, you may have blind spots that need better focus.*

When I was a language arts teacher, I would walk my students through a series of practices on identifying their surroundings and writing down the details. You could try it right now. Take a moment to pause and consider the following:

What are you seeing? Look up, down, around, and behind you. Are you seeing the glare of sunlight from a nearby window? Or maybe it's the stained surface of a tabletop. Could it be a yellow painted wall holding a framed photo?

What are you hearing? Stop and simply listen. Maybe you hear the buzzing of a heating or air system from nearby vents. Or do you recognize the distant hum of passing traffic?

What do you smell? Are you surrounded by the scent of brewed coffee or a mix of aromas coming from a busy kitchen? Or maybe you smell the mustiness of old books.

What are you touching? Your body is full of nerves. Can you feel the fabric of the shirt you're wearing resting on your shoulders? Or how about the press of your shoes against your toes? Are you holding the smooth ridges of a pen in hand?

What are you tasting? Maybe it's the sweetness of gum or the caramel flavorings of your favorite soda? Or it could be the aftertaste of your most recent snack.

What are you sensing emotionally? Are you anxious? Excited? worried? Do you have a sense of confidence or angst for the day ahead? Or maybe you're tired from a short night of sleep, or hungry for your next meal.

It is easy to step into your day with a list of to-dos and fail to see what is right around you or even what is happening inside your own brain. Sometimes, it takes real effort to pause and reflect on your surroundings. But being mindful is important, not just in writing but in being educators.

What is Education Leadership?

I believe all educators are leaders, whether you are leading students or adults. Leadership is an interesting and popular word. It is used in a lot of inspirational quotes, as titles for books, in website descriptions, and conference themes. But leadership is much more than a word. Leadership is influence. It means helping others achieve more. It is taking someone from one location to another or motivating someone to do what she otherwise would not accomplish on her own.

But leadership is much more than a word. Leadership is influence. It means helping others achieve more.

There is something else about leadership I'd like you to think about. Leadership is about those whom you are leading. Whether you are leading students, teachers, co-workers, employees, or team members, each person you lead is a future leader.

Someday, your influence, motivation, presence or input will no longer be immediately present. When that happens, the question will be: How have you intentionally influenced the leadership potential in those whom you lead so that they can in turn lead in their own areas of influence?

Being a Person of Influence

Think about a person who has been one of the most meaningful leaders in your life. Maybe it is a parent, a coach, an administrator, a teacher or a counselor. I bet it is safe to say that he or she paid attention to details you did not see. Maybe that leader had the ability to look at life or scenarios from a perspective that helped you reimagine, redesign, or reprioritize your outcomes.

Influential leaders see or hear what others may be missing. That's why even professionals at the top of their game, like Howard Schultz, the former CEO of Starbucks, or NBA star Kevin Durant, hire others to personally consult or train them (PackPride, 2014). Whether you are leading children or adults, you are an influencer. And the ability to see what others are missing is an important quality in strong leadership.

6 Ways to Invest in Future Leaders

How can you take an active role in maximizing the leadership growth in those whom you're serving? Here are six ways to stay mindful of how you are influencing future leaders:

1. Don't make decisions in a vacuum.

The decisions you are making for others are too important to assume you don 't need their feedback during the process. Yes, it can be messy and take more time to reach out for shared agreements, but when you reach out to others for input, you create a culture of collaboration.

For instance, at the end of my first year of teaching, I surveyed my students to ask them how I could become a better teacher. Over the years, my students helped guide me as much as any evaluation or observation I received.

When I became an administrator, before a scheduled faculty meeting at my school, I would normally consult with a team of teacher leaders. We would meet in a small group the week before so that I could ask them what questions, issues, or concerns needed to be addressed. Together we could brainstorm ideas that gave me a sense of what items were important enough to meet about as a large group. Of course, I had suggestions on items that met the strategic goals we had set for the year. But making decisions with the input of others makes for stronger decisions.

The same is true for those of you who lead school teams. Input from the perspective of those normally outside of the classroom (like other administrators, counselors, and office staff) is just as important as those inside of the classroom. And just as important, you should have scheduled times with student leaders. As a principal, for instance, I would try to meet with a group of student leaders on a weekly basis for their input and feedback. Yes, it takes more time to gather input from others, but when you do, it increases the possibilities of reaching shared goals. And just as importantly, you are raising future leaders by modeling the contexts of good decision making.

2. Give others the ability to lead and the freedom to make mistakes. When you are responsible for a task, it is sometimes difficult to pass it to someone else. Sometimes it is hard because teaching takes time. But if you are not learning to delegate, you will eventually drop the ball on some important tasks. The good news is that others on your team, including students and staff, may be more talented than you are at the tasks you are doing.

One year, an assistant principal on my team asked me if she could manage the task of sending out a weekly "Friday Wrap-Up" email to all of our teachers and staff. This was a great way to summarize positive accomplishments from the previous week and to remind them of important dates or activities in the week ahead. The first few times, she touched base with me for feedback before sending out the messages. But over time, she owned the process. She was not only entrusted to accomplish the task with her own style, but frankly, she did a better job than I would have.

For years, I trained senior students to lead our school's daily announcements. By delegating tasks, you are not sacrificing control. If done with feedback and direction, you are freeing yourself to do other tasks that better fit your expertise and skill set. Delegation takes more time on the front end to teach and guide practices. But in the long run, you're not just benefiting yourself, you're building leadership within others. You are entrusting others with the ability to lead and influence in their areas of strength and talents.

3. Redirect feedback toward a "What can you do about it?" outcome.
I'd like to share ideas from a method I've heard authors Todd Whitaker and Dave Ramsey refer to as "shifting the monkey." The idea is that when someone comes to see you with a concern or an idea for new action, listen politely as the "monkey" of an idea jumps around the room and lands on your shoulder. Then take a moment to pick up the proverbial monkey and place it back on that person's shoulders. Also, don't allow good ideas to burden those on your team who already have their plates full. Learn to help others carry out the tasks they see as important areas of improvement (Ramsey, 2011).

This idea may be used with students or other educators. One day, for example, a teacher visited me with an idea for a new assembly to recognize every senior who is accepting a post-secondary scholarship offer. It was a great idea. First, I thanked him for the idea. Then I asked him what he could do to help turn this idea into a reality. He brainstormed ideas with me until he had a game plan for scheduling the event, gathering helpers, contacting participants, preparing awards, and giving me a time-line for completion. By "shifting the monkey" back to others on your team, you are entrusting them to navigate the pitfalls, identify game plans, and execute plans of action. In the process, you are also giving them a leadership role in accomplishing an area needing improvement.

Not all ideas need to be turned into actions. But whether you are dealing with negative feedback or simply letting someone vent frustrations, if possible, explore ways she can be part of providing the solution.

4. Confront important realities with confidence and grace.

Recently, I was presenting to a group of educators about having difficult conversations. The question was asked about how a leader could keep from upsetting others. The short answer is you cannot lead without upsetting others.

> You can learn to talk honestly to others while treating them with grace and dignity. But how others respond to honest feedback is their choice, not yours.

I told the group that in my former education assignment, it was common to have at least one student, teacher, parent, or co-worker crying in my presence on a daily basis. One educator in the group expressed surprise, and said, "I can't imagine that happening. You seem so easy-going." Here's the lesson. In most of those situations, I had little control over the emotions of my students or colleagues. What I could control was my response to their emotions. You can learn to talk honestly to others while treating them with grace and dignity. But how others respond to honest feedback is their choice, not yours.

Holding others accountable is seldom easy. But if you care about others, you will model providing honest feedback with grace and dignity. And in the process, you will cultivate the ability in them to do the same. If you want a great resource on developing skills in difficult conversations, check out the book *Having Hard Conversations* by Jennifer Abrams (Abrams, 2009).

5. Be generous with sharing lessons learned.

When I was fourteen years old, I became my dad's new assistant during the summers. Before that, my older brothers had worked with him, but they had each moved to their own jobs. My dad spent many weekends in the Kentucky Lake area diving for mussel shells.

One afternoon, I was helping him on the diving boat when a storm surprised us. Within minutes, rain was pouring down, and the sky was filled with lightning and thunder. As the waves increased, my dad fired up the boat motor so we could head for shore. But soon, it began to sputter, and my dad said, "We're running out of gas. Change out the gas tank in back with the spare one that is full."

I jumped to the back of the boat and stood there thinking. I had never changed out a gas tank before, so I started grabbing at hoses but couldn't figure out what to do. Soon the boat stopped.

My dad sprang to my side, "What are you doing?" he said.

"I don't know how to change out a tank," I said.

"Goodness, gracious!" he shouted and reached down to pinch the connecting gas valves and complete the switch.

After we had made it to shore and the storm had subsided, we sat and watched the water lapping against the shore. My dad turned to me and said, "I didn't know you couldn't switch tanks."

I explained that my big brothers had always done that—as well as most other tasks—and no one had ever showed me how.

So, over the next days and weeks together, my dad slowed down when we were working together. He showed me how to maintenance a motor, fix a flat tire, change the truck's oil, and record business expenses. He modeled the work for me. Later, when I was in college, I bought my own diving rig to use in the summers to earn extra money. My dad's leadership had prepared me to do work by sharing the how-to's with me along the way.

As you lead others, take time to slow down and help them understand your practices. Several months ago, I visited a turnaround high school with Principal Mike Crase, at East Central High School in Tulsa, Oklahoma. During his first three years there, East Central High School, an urban school and Title-I school, had improved its graduation rate from 50% to more than 80%. As I walked the building with Mike, here is what I saw happening among his fellow administrators and teachers:

- Team members sharing with others through explaining a process
- Adults touching base with students for feedback
- School members asking parents for their input
- Staff and teachers committed to establishing norms for safe and productive learning environments (PMP:113, 2018).

Think about ways you can share leadership lessons with others. Perhaps you're a gifted writer. If so, consider sharing an article or blog post with others in your professional organizations. What teaching practice do you have that would help others? Consider presenting at an upcoming conference or workshop. Yes, it takes time to teach others. But when you do, you are collaboratively accomplishing the work ahead.

6. Don't forget to invest in your own children as future leaders too.
If you're a parent, let me suggest some practices to keep in mind for the most important future leaders in your life: your own children. One of the greatest joys I had in school leadership was having my own children at my high school. Our morning commutes were sometimes sleepy and quiet. Other times, we would listen to leadership podcast episodes or audio books that could spark important conversations about their personal growth. Our late-night events also provided me time for one-on-one meals or talks on the drive home.

Now that I'm no longer leading their schools, I still enjoy being with my own children, but I have to stay intentional in the ways we engage. The same lessons we apply in school leadership apply in leading our own children. As my children have grown older, scheduling time together has become more difficult because of their various schedules. But creating touchpoints for your children is important if you want to influence their future leadership.

Here's one suggestion: Whenever possible, eat meals together. Anne Fishel, in her blog Theconversation.com, summarizes a number of research sources showing the benefits of family meals for children.

Did you know that children who regularly enjoy family meals have increased vocabularies, eat more balanced diets, generally perform better in school, and show fewer signs of anxiety and depression? (Fishel, 2009). In addition to mealtimes, here are some practices we have established as a family that may inspire ideas for yours. If you're not a parent, these ideas may be helpful for those important relationships where you are looking for ways to build up the next generation:

- **Reading together or watching movies together**: I don't do this as much now that my kids are older, but for years, we had book time. When they were little, it was story books. As they grew older, we read entire novels or series together. Living adventures together gives you more time and a lot to talk about. Now that our children are older, we do this a lot more through movie times.
- **Half-birthday dates and special occasions**: At our home, every kid gets a half-birthday celebration each year. That child decides what he or she wants to do, and he or she can spend an entire afternoon or evening just being together with mom or dad.
- **Special milestones**: At various ages, we also give each child an out-of-town weekend away. And for certain milestones, we treat them to fancy date nights. Be creative; have fun.

Each of these times can serve as a focus on the kinds of life lessons you want your kids to learn and understand as they are developing through childhood, adolescence, and adulthood. You can talk about everything from goal setting to understanding how to make wise choices in health and wellness. Although you can never guarantee the outcomes, the time invested in your own children is worth the effort as you build future leaders at your school.

Let's Wrap This Up

Jen Schwanke is the author of the book *You're the Principal! Now What?* As a practicing principal, she once sat on an interview committee that presented the following scenario to candidates: You are standing in the main office holding a stack of forms that need to be signed when a teacher comes in and says she wants to talk about an idea for her afternoon class. The phone rings, and your secretary tells you it's the superintendent—he wants to talk to you right away. At the exact same time, a student walks in and heads toward the clinic; he is crying and red-faced. What do you do?' She concludes: "Candidates that chose any option other helping the child were not considered" (Schwanke, page 46).

Her point? Leadership is—and must always be—about students. I agree. But I have to be honest. In my leadership experiences, sometimes I have failed to be mindful of those around me, including students. My bet is that you have not always served perfectly either.

If you are like me, sometimes you need a reminder to stop and pay close attention to the future leaders around you every day—whether that includes students, fellow teachers, or even family members. As you serve them, remember to include them in the decision-making process. Give them the ability to lead and make mistakes to help them see how to become part of the solutions. Hold them accountable with confidence and grace, and generously model for them what you expect from them. As you do, you'll find yourself not just leading others, but investing in future leaders.

Now It's Your Turn

This week, will you take time to closely observe your surroundings? Think about someone in your school or on your team who could benefit from positive feedback. How can you include others while making decisions this week? What role can students play in providing leadership for their own learning?

CHAPTER 10

Your Legacy

What Will Others Say About You?

The Tombstone: *I haven't decided where I will be buried, but I have thought about what I'd like written on my tombstone. If your friends and family could summarize your life with a sentence, what might they say? Even though most of us won't see our names remembered a hundred years after we are gone, we can leave a legacy by the way we influence others.*

In 2017 the United States mourned the passing of Arizona Senator John McCain. Before his death, Senator McCain was asked by a reporter what words he hoped to see on his tombstone. He replied, "I've been a small bit of American history, so I think if there's something on my tombstone, it'll be, 'He served his country,' and hopefully you add one word, 'honorably,'" (Donachie, 2017).

How do you judge endings? In his book *When: The Scientific Secrets of Perfect Timing*, Daniel Pink explains research by behavioral scientists that study how people evaluate the moral behavior of others. In this study, researchers created two versions of a man named Jim. In the first version, Jim is a successful CEO who for decades is kind to his employees, generous with his time and money, and lives a life full of service to others. However, in the last five years of his life, he becomes greedy, vindictive, and a moral failure.

The second version of Jim is also a CEO, but for decades, he lives a life of self-interest, takes advantage of his employees, and is stingy and greedy. But in the last five years of his life, Jim turns a corner, becomes a man of generosity, kindness, and benevolence. Which man lived the better life?

In the research, participants overwhelmingly chose the second Jim. Why? Because people instinctively believe that the ending is what counts. Daniel Pink calls this the "end coding." And sometimes we have a tendency to overestimate the importance of endings in the ways we think (Pink, 2019).

I have to admit when I read the accounts, I was confronted with my own mindset about how one's story ends. I am disappointed when a person whom I admire has a failure in terms of trustworthiness—especially when it happens at the end of his or her life. But I have never paused to ask myself *why* the ending to me is equally (or more) important as the entire story.

How Do Your Experiences Change You?

I believe that part of the reason people "end-code" is that we associate character with external circumstances like how someone responds to adversity or success. Michelle Obama once said, "Being president doesn't change who you are, it reveals who you are," (Halloran, 2012).

First Lady Obama's quote is a good reminder that circumstances often reveal, not merely shape, who we are. But with all due respect, I would still argue that experiences can also change you.

For example, I remember the first time I managed a situation involving criminal activity on a school campus as the school administrator. I was young, with little experience in investigation or interrogation. Sure, I had spent more than a decade in the classroom, but it was different managing school-wide policy while confronting street-smart kids—some of whom also had parents who enjoyed calling in powerful attorneys. In the classroom, I had dealt with isolated crisis situations. But in the office, I had a new perspective on day-to-day situations that brought me face-to-face with some of the worst cases of human behavior in the school—sometimes involving student misdeeds and other times involving the student's own parents or guardians.

As a result, I found myself changing. Whereas I once thought of myself as a naturally trusting person, I began to form a wariness and distrust of others. While I had once thought it easy to explain the rules as I did in my previous classroom experience, I now saw how others could manipulate or challenge policy on a larger scale with questions on technicalities or threats of lawsuits. Over time, I found myself becoming defensive, somewhat paranoid, and often angry. When I received my first death threat, for instance, I realized I had crossed into a new reality of experience as an educator.

How are You Responding to the Ups and Downs of Your Experiences?

As I've explained before, I almost gave up on a career in education. But as I grew in my role as a school administrator, a shift occurred. I started changing my focus to areas outside of the more difficult parts of my work. I had also gained new skills in managing difficulties in my new role. Additionally, I realized I couldn't allow the very small percentage of tough cases in my job description to define or overwhelm the vast majority of the positives happening there.

Even though I was able to come through those experiences with new perspectives, I don't believe I stayed the same person. I was no longer as naïve to the many challenges being faced by students and teachers on a school-wide basis. I was no longer convinced that schoolwide decision-making was an easy process of just opening up a policy manual and following the directions. And in some ways, I probably became a bit callous or insensitive. Like most people, I'm sure I unknowingly developed other traits, good and bad, which have inevitably influenced who I am as a person today.

5 Thoughts to Consider for Leaving Your Legacy

I am telling these stories because I believe all educators share common lessons. No matter if you are beginning your career or entering your second decade as an educator, each of your experiences shape and change you. The challenge is learning to pause, breathe, and reflect on what you are learning so that the outcomes can become positive for you and for others. Although our endings don't completely define who we are, our endings *do* matter. And if the debate is whether a life well lived or the ending matters most, I imagine the answer is somewhere in the middle. Taking a closer look at the end of a story is difficult if you are in the middle of it, but I believe each of us has a longing for our endings to be good ones.

So, let's reflect on this final chapter together. How do you think you will look back on your own experiences as an educator many years hence? It is sometimes hard to see what kind of legacy you are building. But you are indeed building a legacy: You are leaving behind stories, experiences, and relationships that reflect your influence. As you think about your legacy, I'd like to offer five ideas to keep in mind:

1. Remember you are *not* as important as you think you are.

I'm not sure I've ever heard these words used as an inspiration. But they are true. One of the pitfalls of being human is believing you are better than you really are. Someday, your school will exist without you. And the stories of your time there will fade with each passing year. I am not saying you are not important. I am saying you play one role out of many that make up your school's community.

One of the ultimate goals of education is the ability to step away and watch others thrive and excel without your input. Keep your focus on serving others and celebrating their wins. In the process, don't allow those successes to give you a false sense of self-importance. You cannot serve others if your ego drives your decision-making. In Jim Collins's book *Good to Great* he highlights successful businesses throughout the history of the United States. One trait among the CEO's leading these companies was their ability to quietly influence employees without an interest in taking credit for the successes. "The good-to-great leaders never wanted to become larger-than-life heroes. They never aspired to be put on a pedestal or become unreachable icons. They were seemingly ordinary people quietly producing extraordinary results..." (Collins, 2020, para. 3). If you want to leave a legacy, maintain your perspective on serving others.

2. Remember you *are* more important than you think.

At the risk of contradicting the last point, let me explain this statement. Another pitfall educators tend to make is underestimating their influence on others. You never have the luxury of compromising your core values. Trust is one of the most essential qualities of building thriving learning communities. When you break or violate trust, you damage everyone else in the community. The little things you do, the way you treat others, how you listen and include input, the concern and generosity you demonstrate, all demonstrate and model what you expect to see in others.

Don't be fooled by a world that no longer seems to believe integrity matters in authority figures. Your students and fellow educators know who the real deal is, and they will respect or disrespect you on the extent to which your own actions reflect the values and behaviors you are asking of them.

3. Remember relationships are more important than anything else.
Last week, I heard a veteran educator explain that you must be friendly with everyone you serve but you cannot be friends with everyone you serve. This is a good reminder that education places you in an important but uncomfortable role. As you inspire learning, teach standards, maintain calendars, collaborate with others, or ask others to follow you through difficult situations and challenges, people trust you more. In the end, if they believe you care about them, they may not always agree with you, but they will respect you.

> No amount of policy change, strategy building, professional-collaboration, or curriculum development can improve student learning while absent of meaningful relationships.

Trust is built through relationships. No amount of policy change, strategy building, professional-collaboration, or curriculum development can improve student learning while absent of meaningful relationships. Relationships build a culture where learning and growth thrive.

Being focused on relationships does not mean compromising standards, policies, or expectations. It means you learn to build others up even while holding them accountable for their performance. At the end of the day, your toughest decisions will be easier to live with when you know you went out of your way to assure others they were important and mattered in the process.

4. Remember courageous decisions mean you will inspire some and disappoint others.

You cannot serve others without making some people upset. If your goal is to keep everyone happy, then you will be unable to challenge learning, protect students, or maintain high standards for fear of upsetting people who require accountability. Accept the reality that it is okay to disappoint some while inspiring others.

When you make decisions based on what is best for your highest-performing students or fellow educators, you raise the tide for everyone else. You also keep from worrying all the time about what will upset those who default toward complaining. Good decision-making will inspire confidence in the majority of those you serve, and you will leave a legacy of building more celebrations than regrets.

5. Remember you never arrive and must keep learning.

Whatever you learn along the way, tomorrow is always a new day. In year twenty-five of my educational career, I still have as much to learn as in my first year. Just a few days ago, I asked my son to teach me how to play a new video game. I didn't ask because I wanted to learn how to play video games. I asked because I wanted to understand his world of play. And in the process, I was inspired and captivated by what I learned.

The world is constantly changing for all of us, but we live in an exciting time in which we can be discoverers, creators, and innovators. If you fail to stay inspired to learn new ideas or processes, you will fail to inspire others to do the same. Keep an open mind to learning and embracing new ideas. When you do, you'll help build a stronger culture of learning.

Let's Wrap This Up

Lux Nayran gave a TedTalk in 2017, explaining an interesting discovering he made while analyzing 2,000 obituaries in the *New York Times*. He took every common word used in those statements about the random lives of people, and he placed those words in a word puzzle that assigned larger text to the words used most often and smaller text to the words used less often. Want to guess which word stood out larger than every other? *Help* (Nayran, 2017). You may have many ways you want to be remembered. Maybe you want people to remember you as a great teacher, a talented musician, or a witty conversationalist. But what will people most likely remember about you? They will remember if you helped them. A life well lived is one lived helping others.

Now It's Your Turn

What kind of legacy do you want to leave behind? What do you want to be written on your tombstone? My hope is that as you've read this book, each chapter has given you pause. That you have taken time to reflect on your priorities. And that your commitment to serving others allows you the ability to thrive in your important work as an educator.

As you stay humble, use your influence for good, build meaningful relationships, make courageous decisions, and maintain a hunger for learning, you will touch the lives of others in hidden ways, which may continue for generations to come. Ultimately, you cannot completely control the ending of your story. But you can remember what matters most: helping others. And if you're lucky, like John McCain, you may do so honorably. And that's what a legacy is really all about.

Your Laughter

How Is the Power of Play Influencing Your Leadership?

The Power of Play: *Children experience joy when they are allowed the freedom to explore, create, and just have fun. When we become too serious in our work or lives, we run the risk of missing out on an essential part of ourselves and those around us. Lighten up and look for the joy in moments. Especially in the hard work of teaching and leading, you can only encourage others when you find joy in your journey.*

W hen I spotted the mud puddle, I thought it would be fun to jump in it. The dirt road that ran along the edge of the field by our West Tennessee farmhouse was often traveled by trucks and tractors. And the ruts in the sandy, red dirt would fill with rain and create long stretches of rust-colored puddles. I was barefoot and seven years old. My brothers and sister were with me.

"Watch this," I said. And I ran and jumped.

My feet landed in the thick mud, and streaks of red clay splattered across my legs and shorts. They laughed. And soon, one by one, each of them tried it too.

"I think you could paint with this mud," my sister said.

"Oh, yeah? I bet it would look good painted on you!"

And the mud battle began. Fists full of Tennessee red clay were thrown and splattered.

And we chased one another until my oldest brother said, "You know, in ancient times, people would bathe in mud as a way to treat their skin."

He slowly began smearing it on his arms, his neck, his face, his legs. We followed suit. And before long, we were covered from head to toe in the red earth.

How Play Encourages Innovation

I was thinking back to this moment after reading the first two chapters of Tony Wagner's *Creating Innovators: The Making of Young People Who Will Change the World*. Wagner makes a persuasive argument that without creativity, people lack the ideas, initiative, and motivation for extraordinary achievements. In the book, he looks at the lives of some of the most successful people in industry, science, and the arts—people who seem to possess qualities that motivate them to do extraordinary things for rewards far greater than pay or recognition. These people are

> without creativity, people lack the ideas, initiative, and motivation for extraordinary achievements.

motivated by the wonder and joy of learning. In all the attributes Wagner identifies among these most creative and innovative minds, one trait stands out: play.

Play Influences Student Learning

Play isn't just good for our mental health. It also provides context that encourages creativity, teamwork, and a sense of accomplishment. And it's not just something that motivates small children. People of all ages find motivation through playing. Take this description of the long-standing tradition of pranks at MIT that Tony Wagner explains:

Joost Bonsen, who is an alumnus of the Massachusetts Institute of Technology and currently serves as a lecturer in the world-famous MIT Media Lab, talked about the importance of the famous tradition of pranks at the university. *'Being innovative is central to being human.' Bonsen told me. 'We're curious and playful animals, until it's pounded out of us. Look at the tradition of pranks here at MIT. What did it take to put a police car on a dome that was fifteen stories high [one of most famous MIT student pranks], with a locked trapdoor being the only access? It was an incredible engineering feat. To pull that off was a systems problem, and it took tremendous leadership and teamwork. 'Pranks reinforce the cultural ethos of creative joy.' Joost added. 'Getting something done in a short period of time with no budget, and challenging circumstances. It's glorious and epic. They didn't ask for permission. Not even forgiveness.'*

[Wagner concludes:] These students were playing — just doing something for the fun of it. Play, then, is part of our human nature and an intrinsic motivation, (Wagner, 2015, p. 27).

Why are We Not Playing More?

You would think that playing is something all children enjoy, but in a world that prizes protection and safety, many of our kids are missing out on the freedom and space they need to be able to play. They are also experiencing increased stress and anxiety. In Tim Elmore's Ebook, *Help Teens Manage Stress & Anxiety*, he discusses how these trends are playing out in surveys with college students.

Elmore shares the results of a report from the American College Health Association, which gives these sobering statistics about university students:

- *94% said the top word they use to describe their life was 'overwhelmed.'*
- *44% said it was difficult to even function.*
- *Nearly one in ten had thought about suicide in the last year.*

When Elmore offered a number of responses to the growing anxiety among youth, guess what one of his many suggestions was? Play. Elmore adds, "Even technology wizards—perhaps especially tech wizards—know the secret of living well is to get off a screen for the better part of a day. Play. Go outside. Be with people face to face. Talk. Listen. Run. Walk. Tumble. Skin your knee," (Elmore, p. 36).

Teachers of Innovation

If our schools are to be places that allow for creativity, innovation, and exploration, then how do we encourage elements of discovery, competition, and wonder? Don Wettrick is an educator who authentically engages students in active innovation. He is also a podcaster, presenter, and innovator of his own projects. And his *StartEdUp Innovation* website is chock full of interviews, ideas, and products that help teachers and students practice innovation, entrepreneurship, and technology-rich learning experiences (Wettrick).

Don is not alone. He is part of a growing number of educators who coach students through projects where they encounter real-life scenarios for solving problems or creating products. They connect students with top innovators and business leaders through virtual meet-ups. And then, they provide students with the direction, access, resources, and collaboration for turning their ideas into tools, websites, businesses, or movements. You may be aware of other innovative approaches such as schools using Genius Hours, STEM labs, and Makerspaces, all of which involve real-life application.

Play in Your Role as an Educator

As I wrote the final chapter of this book, I couldn't help but think about the importance laughter has played in my education experience. If you have read this far, this epilogue is bonus material that may be the most lasting takeaway. As a classroom teacher, I enjoyed learning. When my language arts students read plays or short stories, I read along with them. I often took parts as well, using a bad British accent or a deep Southern drawl. But we also wrote our own stories. And as we did, we learned together, shared them with one another, and celebrated the moments. Today you can encourage publishing through podcasts, blogs, or You-Tube channels.

When I became a school administrator, for the first few years, I felt the creativity inside of me dying. I was so overwhelmed with school management I was quickly losing the joy in my work. But over time, I began to rediscover the joys of school: engaging with students and teachers while they learned, including asking for their input in school communications and asking them for feedback on ways we could improve. Slowly, I began to find ways to embed "playing" into my new role in education. Creativity is a mindset, and you must stay intentional to embed play into your practices.

7 Ways for Educators to Maintain a Playful Mindset

Here are seven quick suggestions for keeping a mindset of playfulness:

1. Turn problem-solving into puzzle-solving.
Don't look at every problem as a distraction from work that needs to be done. Look at solving challenges as finding better ways to enjoy learning. Every day you face situations where others ask for your input or you encounter scenarios you've never had to manage before. As you do, you can learn to find energy and joy in collaborating with others for innovative solutions.

One year, for instance, when our school decided to implement a new remediation schedule, I knew I could not pull the task off alone. We solicited input from a team of teacher advisors, and my administrative assistants took the lead with this group. They created sample schedules that we beta-tested a semester in advance of implementation. Even though I switched roles at the end of the year, I visited during remediation to see the schedules and plans put into action. The final solution did not come top-down; it came through sharing the problem-solving with a team of others who saw it as a puzzle to be solved.

2. Make it a goal to build up when you find things falling apart.
Whenever you encounter failure in a student or fellow educator, remember you've failed before, too. This mindset keeps you engaged when helping turn disappointments into stepping stones. Difficult moments can often derail us from important tasks. But here's a secret to not being upset or angry when disappointed: Embrace the moment as best as you can. See these critical moments as ways to make something better in the end. Your attitude, even in the worst moments, sets the tone or atmosphere for others to emulate. And a positive outlook makes difficult situations easier to bear.

3. Stay mindful as you observe and interact with learning.

When you are busy, it is easy to miss what is right in front of you or fail to show gratitude and perspective. Keep your eyes and ears open for the expressions, actions, emotions, and conversations of those around you. Take time to make eye contact. Ask yourself if you really understand what is happening and whether you may be missing something obvious that others see. Look for opportunities to show gratitude to others. This kind of mindset allows you to recognize the small moments that collectively create big outcomes for your school.

4. Connect and laugh with teammates and students.

Isolation is the enemy of excellence, and you cannot risk missing out on the most important assets in your school: people. Take the time to listen to the wins and losses of those around you. Celebrate the victories you see in learning, activities, and sports. And take time to find the joy and humor in the small moments of your day. One time, a high school student brought me a Barbie Valentine card with a sticker I could wear on my shirt. We had a lot of good laughs that day as I wore it around school. Have fun together. Life is too short to not take the time to laugh at yourself and enjoy others.

5. Engage in creative projects with students or teachers.

Your teachers and students have some amazing ideas. Let them create and share ideas from their own experiences or classrooms. Capture learning moments via videos to share with others. Travel with students on field trips. Don't just watch learning take place. Engage in the learning moments with your students! It will make teaching or classroom observations much more fun.

6. Develop your own passion projects.

I began blogging and podcasting while leading a school. It took time outside of my school day, but I found a lot of joy in sharing the experiences of my school. I also love to write and play music. So, I engage in that hobby too. Working on passion projects not only keeps you innovative but also influences the work you do with others. You are more inspiring when you are inspired.

7. Stop taking yourself so seriously. You may be prone to being highly driven, which is normal for educators. But being excellent should not make you obnoxious. Remember the bigger picture: Most problems are small ones. Most challenges are temporary. And most obstacles can be overcome. When you can't conquer a problem or win a battle, give yourself space and grace. And remember to celebrate. Your students and colleagues need to know that high expectations don't mean you expect perfection. And they'll love you more when you stop trying to be perfect yourself.

> Remember the bigger picture: Most problems are small ones. Most challenges are temporary. And most obstacles can be overcome.

Let's Wrap This Up

I can still remember when my mother stepped away from the flower bed in our yard as she saw her mud-covered children returning from the field road. She stood with hands on her hips, but she didn't scold us. Instead, she smiled and told us to head to the creek to wash off before bringing our clothes to the water hose for rinsing.

As we made our way to the water, I could feel the mud's texture drying. I rubbed at some of the dirt, and it crumbled into reddish dust. I looked at my siblings as we started washing. We were a motley crew, the whites of our eyes and teeth standing out against the muddy smears. We were a mess, but soon, we were rinsed and heading home.

Part of the joy and adventure of childhood is being able to make the most of the messy moments. As you think about this school year, give yourself, your students, and your fellow educators permission to try, to fail, and to play. Encourage creativity. Celebrate the moments when learning takes place. And while you're at it, think about how to keep your creativity alive too. When you do, you may get your hands muddy along the way, but it is so worth maintaining the joy of learning. May you find these lessons a good reminder every day to pause, breathe, and flourish.

Now It's Your Turn

How can you encourage playfulness in your students and teachers? What is one way you can recognize creativity in your students and teammates? How can you celebrate moments of discovery and innovation? What projects can you commit to this year that encourage your love of learning?

References
and Resources

Introduction

Wang, Karla. "Teacher Turnover: Why It's Problematic and How Administrators Can Address It." SciLearn.com, July 2019, www.scilearn.com/teacher-turnover/.

Hull, Jim. "The Principal Perspective: at a Glance." *Centerforpubliceducation.org*, Apr. 2012, www.centerforpubliceducation.org/research/principal-perspective-glance.

Chapter 1

"Youth Physical Activity: The Role of Schools." *www.cdc.gov*, U.S. Department of Health and Human Services Centers for Disease Control and Prevention National Center for Chronic Disease Prevention and Health Promotion Division of Adolescent and School Health, Aug. 2009, www.cdc.gov/healthy-schools/physicalactivity/toolkit/factsheet_pa_guidelines_schools.pdf.

Chapter 2

Bauer, Daniel. "Better Leaders Better Schools Podcast." *Better Leaders Better Schools*, 9 Mar. 2019, betterleadersbetterschools.com/.

Baeder, Justin. "Principal Center Radio Podcast." *The Principal Center*, 3 Mar. 2019, www.principalcenter.com/radio/.

Davis, Vicki. "10 Minute Teacher Podcast." *10 Minute Teacher Podcast*, 17 July 2020, https://10minuteteacher.libsyn.com.

Dweck, Carol S. *Mindset: The New Psychology of Success, How We Can Learn to Fulfill Our Potential.* Ballantine Books, New York, 2007.

Gladwell, Malcolm. *Outliers: The Story of Success.* Back Bay Books, Little, Brown and Company, 2013.

Hall, Pete, and Alisa Simeral. *Building Teachers' Capacity for Success: A Collaborative Approach for Coaches and School Leaders.* Association for Supervision and Curriculum Development, Alexandria, Virginia, 2008.

Jones, Jethro. "Transformative Principal with Jethro Jones." *Transformative Principal*, 3 Mar. 2019, www.transformativeprincipal.org/.

Landau, Elizabeth. "Music: It's in Your Head, Changing Your Brain." *CNN*, Cable News Network, 28 May 2012, www.cnn.com/2012/05/26/health/mental-health/music-brain-science/.

Levitin, Daniel J. *Why It's So Hard To Pay Attention, Explained By Science.* Fast Company, 23 Sept. 2015, www.fastcompany.com/3051417/why-its-so-hard-to-pay-attention-explained-by-science.

McCullough, David G. *The Wright Brothers.* Simon & Schuster Audio, 2015.

Parker, William D. "Principal Matters Podcast." *Principal Matters*, 9 Mar. 2019, www.williamdparker.com/.

Sauer, Alissa. "5 Reasons Why Music Boosts Brain Activity." *Alzheimers. net*, 21 July 2014, www.alzheimers.net/why-music-boosts-brain-activity-in-dementia-patients/.

Wettrick, Don. "The StartEdUp Podcast." *StartedUp Innovation*, 17 July 2020, http://www.startedupinnovation.com/podcast.

Chapter 3

Collins, Jim. *Good to Great: Why Some Companies Make the Leap ... and Others Don't*. Random House Business Books, 2001.

Cummings, Lily. Personal letter shared via Facebook. Skiatook, Oklahoma. July 2017.

Gordon, Jon. *The Energy Bus: 10 Rules to Fuel Your Life, Work, and Team with Positive Energy*. Wiley, 2015.

NAESP and NASSP. "Linking Principal Leadership and Student Learning." *Leadership Matters*, 2013, Accessed at: www.naesp.org/sites/default/files/LeadershipMatters.pdf on March 9, 2019.

Wallace Foundation. (2011). The school principal as leader: Guiding schools to better teaching and learning. Accessed at http://www.wallacefoundation.org/knowledge-center/school -leadership/effective-principal-leadership/Documents/The-School -Principal-as-Leader-Guiding-Schools-to-Better-Teaching-and -Learning.pdf on March 9, 2019.

Chapter 4

Adams, Bryan. "How Google's 20 Percent Rule Can Make You More Productive and Energetic." *Inc.com*, Inc., 28 Dec. 2016, https://www.inc.com/bryan-adams/12-ways-to-encourage-more-free-thinking-and-innovation-in-to-any-business.html.

Grissom, Jason, et al. "Principal Time Management Skills: Explaining Patterns in Principals." *Journal of Educational Administration*, 1 Oct. 2015, https://cepa.stanford.edu/content/principal-time-management-skills-explaining-patterns-principals-time-use-job-stress-and-perceived-effectiveness.

Smith, Robert D. *20,000 Days and Counting: the Crash Course for Mastering Your Life Right Now*. Thomas Nelson, 2013.

Chapter 5

Keller, Timothy. *The Prodigal God: Recovering the Heart of the Christian Faith*. Penguin Books, 2016.

Nelson, Shasta. *Friendships Don't Just Happen!: The Guide to Creating a Meaningful Circle of Girlfriends*. Turner Publishing Company, 2013.

Pink, Daniel H. *When: The Scientific Secrets of Perfect Timing*. Canongate, 2019.

Schnall, Simone, et al. "Social Support and the Perception of Geographical Slant." *Journal of Experimental Social Psychology*, U.S. National Library of Medicine, 1 Sept. 2008, https://www.ncbi.nlm.nih.gov/pmc/articles/PMC3291107/.

Chapter 6

Goldhill, Olivia. "Psychologists Have Found That a Spiritual Outlook Makes Humans More Resilient to Trauma." *Quartz*, 30 Jan. 2016, https://qz.com/606564/psychologists-have-found-that-a-spiritual-outlook-makes-humans-universally-more-resilient-to-trauma/.

Kaufmann, Scott Barry. "Cultivating Grit from Within." AMLE National Conference, 2017. Speech delivered at Pennsylvania Convention Center. Oct. 2017, Philadelphia.

Mcleod, Saul. "Maslow's Hierarchy of Needs." *Simply Psychology*, Simply Psychology, 21 May 2018, https://www.simplypsychology.org/maslow.html.

Chapter 7

Berman, Jillian. "Student Debt Just Hit $1.5 Trillion." *MarketWatch*, 12 May 2018, https://www.marketwatch.com/story/student-debt-just-hit-15-trillion-2018-05-08.

Blue, Ron, and Jeremy White. *The New Master Your Money: A Step-by-Step Plan for Gaining and Enjoying Financial Freedom*. Moody, 2004.

"Captain Charlie Plumb: Motivational Speaker: Prisoner of War." *Charlie Plumb*, http://charlieplumb.com/.

"Financial Peace University." *Financial Peace University: Manage Your Money Wisely | DaveRamsey.com*, https://www.daveramsey.com/fpu/.

McCall, Michael J.D. "Far From Wall Street Updates." https://www.farfromwallstreet.com/far-from-wall-street-updates/28-who-s-packing-your-parachute Accessed: October 26, 2019.

Chapter 8

Chapman, Gary D., and Jocelyn Green. *The 5 Love Languages: The Secret to Love That Lasts*. Northfield Publishing, 2017.

Gottman, John Mordechai. *A Couples Guide to Communication*. Research Press, 1979.

The Knot. "Traditional Wedding Vows From Various Religions." *Theknot.com*, The Knot, 7 June 2019, https://www.theknot.com/content/traditional-wedding-vows-from-various-religions.

Shmerling, Robert H. "The Health Advantages of Marriage." *Harvard Health Blog*, 18 Nov. 2016, https://www.health.harvard.edu/blog/the-health-advantages-of-marriage-2016113010667.

Chapter 9

Abrams, Jennifer. *Having Hard Conversations*. Corwin, 2009.

Fishel, Anne. "Science Says: Eat with Your Kids." *The Conversation*, 22 Aug. 2019, http://theconversation.com/science-says-eat-with-your-kids-34573.

"PackPride Sports." *Adam Harrington (That One) Is Kevin Durant's Personal Trainer*, 12 Dec. 2014, https://247sports.com/college/north-carolina-state/Board/103752/Contents/Adam-Harrington-that-one-is-Kevin-Durants-personal-trainer-70526466.

"PMP:113 Building Positive School Communities – Interview with Principal Mike Crase." *Principal Matters*, 16 May 2018, https://williamd parker.com/2018/05/16/pmp113-building-positive-school-communities-interview-with-principal-mike-crase/.

Ramsey, Dave. *EntreLeadership: 20 Years of Practical Business Wisdom from the Trenches*. Howard Books, Simon & Shuster, Inc., 2011.

Schaffner, Herb. "Need a Turnaround? Make a Comeback the Starbucks Way." *CBS News*, CBS Interactive, 12 Apr. 2011, https://www.cbsnews.com/news/need-a-turnaround-make-a-comeback-the-starbucks-way/.

Schwanke, Jen. *You're the Principal! Now What?: Strategies and Solutions for New School Leaders*. ASCD, 2016.

Ramsey, Dave. *EntreLeadership: 20 Years of Practical Business Wisdom from the Trenches*. Howard Books, Simon & Shuster, Inc., 2011.

Chapter 10

Donachie, Robert. "McCain Reveals What He Wants On His Tombstone." *The Daily Caller*, The Daily Caller, 29 Nov. 2017, https://dailycaller.com/2017/11/29/mccain-reveals-what-he-wants-on-his-tombstone/.

Halloran, Liz. "Michelle Obama: 'Being President ... Reveals Who You Are.'" *NPR*, NPR, 5 Sept. 2012, https://www.npr.org/sections/itsall-politics/2012/09/04/160581747/michelle-obama-being-president-reveals-who-you-are.

Collins, Jim. *Good to Great: Why Some Companies Make the Leap ... and Others Don't*. Random House Business Books, 2001.

Narayan, Lux. "What I Learned from 2,000 Obituaries." *TED*, https://www.ted.com/talks/lux_narayan_what_i_learned_from_2_000_obituaries/reading-list.

Pink, Daniel H. *When: The Scientific Secrets of Perfect Timing*. Canongate, 2019.

Epilogue

Elmore, Timothy. *Stressed Out. Growing Leaders Youth Leadership Programs*, https://growingleaders.com/free-resources/stressed-out-ebook/.

Wagner, Tony, and Robert A. Compton. *Creating Innovators: The Making of Young People Who Will Change the World*. Scribner, 2015.

Wettrick, Don. "StartEdUp." *StartEdUp*, http://www.startedupinnovation.com/.

Acknowledgements

This book is one that I hope can transcend beyond the work you do as an educator. My hope is that it will be a resource for self-reflection. It is the advice I have tried to follow myself and what I would tell my own children when they begin their own journeys into adulthood. Thank you to the readers of my previous books who have encouraged me to write this one. I am grateful to my wife, Missy, whose friendship and love inspire me to use my gifts to help others. Thank you to my children Emily, Mattie, Katie, and Jack who keep me humble and bring me so much joy. I owe a debt of appreciation to my colleagues at the Cooperative Council for Oklahoma School Administration, and Dr. Pam Deering for providing me ongoing experience in serving educators and allowing me the time to see this book become a reality. And special thanks to my friends Jimmy Casas and Jeff Zoul who encouraged and assisted me in sharing this book with the world. A wise friend once told me, "One good deed is better than a thousand good intentions." May you find one good action from this book that can help you in your journey and help those whom you serve.

About the Author

William D. Parker lives near Tulsa, Oklahoma. He and his wife are the proud parents of four children: three girls and a boy. He is the founder of Principal Matters, LLC, an author, and a speaker who uses his expertise in school leadership, culture, and communication to equip educational leaders with solutions and strategies for motivating students, inspiring teachers, and reaching communities. He also proudly serves as the executive director of Oklahoma's Association of Secondary Principals and also as executive director of Oklahoma's Middle Level Education Association. He is the former principal of Skiatook High School, near Tulsa, Oklahoma. Will writes a weekly blog and hosts the weekly *Principal Matters* podcast for school leaders available at his website: www.williamdparker.com or via iTunes. He is the author of two other books on the topic of school leadership: *Principal Matters: The Motivation, Courage, Action and Teamwork Need for School Leadership (2015, 2017 editions)* and *Messaging Matters: How to Motivate Students, Inspire Teachers and Reach Communities (Solution Tree Press, 2017).*

An Oklahoma educator since 1993, he was named Broken Arrow Public School's South Intermediate High School Teacher of the Year in 1998. He became an assistant principal in 2004 and was named the Oklahoma Assistant Principal of the Year by the National Association of Secondary Principals in 2012. As principal of a Title I school, his school's innovative approaches to collaboration, remediation, and mentoring resulted in marked improvements in student performance. He is regularly asked to present for principal associations, school leadership conferences, and graduate classes on effective leadership practices, organizational management, and strategies for enhancing school communication. Find out more about his presentations and speaking schedule at his website: **williamdparker.com.**

Presentations available from William D. Parker

Messaging Matters: How School Leaders Can Inspire Teachers, Motivate Students, and Reach Communities - Messaging Matters is for educators who want to grow their skills in powerful, intentional communication with students, teachers, and community members. In this session, you will learn what research says about engagement, teamwork, and celebration. In addition, you'll explore specific strategies and digital tools any school leader can use to promote positive school communication and to increase a collaborative culture.

8 Hats for Highly Effective Education Leaders - If you want to be an effective education leader, you must practice highly effective leadership strategies. Explore eight "hats" that all leaders wear, coaching, counseling, accountability, teamwork, and more! Discover practical ways of dealing with difficult people, setting key responsibility areas for your staff, communicating effectively with stakeholders. This presentation has been described by participants as motivating, inspiring, and instructive. Will also explores the importance of self-care and personal development as an essential part of school leadership.

Aspiring Principal Workshops – Are you an aspiring education leader looking to grow your capacity to serve school communities? Learn how emerging leaders can develop the most important elements of engagement, goal setting, interpersonal relationships and teamwork. Prepare yourself for the road ahead by discovering the nuts-and-bolts of school leadership, specific takeaways for future job interviews, and how to evaluate your own leadership style.

Pause. Breathe. Flourish: Living Your Best Life Now as an Educator - This is a collaborative, hands-on, reflective workshop for those who want to really dig deep into the root issues surrounding their motivations for leadership. Will shares ten essential principles all educators need for personal and professional growth. Spend time in guided exploration, discussion, and consultation on goal setting, self-improvement, and strategy discussion on how to avoid burnout and live your best life now as an educator.

More from ConnectEDD Publishing

S ince 2015, ConnectEDD has worked to transform education by empowering educators to become better-equipped to teach, learn, and lead. What started as a small company designed to provide professional learning events for educators has grown to include a variety of services to help teachers and administrators address essential challenges. ConnectEDD offers instructional and leadership coaching, professional development workshops focusing on a variety of educational topics, a roster of nationally-recognized educator associates who possess hands-on knowledge and experience, educational conferences custom-designed to meet the specific needs of schools, districts, and state/national organizations, and ongoing, personalized support, both virtually and onsite. In 2020, ConnectEDD expanded to include publishing services designed to provide busy educators with books and resources consisting of practical information on a wide variety of teaching, learning, and leadership topics.

Visit us online: connecteddpublishing.com

Contact us at info@connecteddpublishing.com

Recent Publications

Live Your Excellence: Action Guide by Jimmy Casas

Culturize: Action Guide by Jimmy Casas

Daily Inspiration for Educators: Positive Thoughts for Every Day of the Year by Jimmy Casas

Eyes on Culture: Multiply Excellence in Your School by Emily Paschall

 ConnectEDD

Made in USA - Kendallville, IN
10793_9781734890846
09.13.2022 1336